POCKET
GARDENING
GUIDES

Cacti &
Succulents

❖

DAVID SQUIRE

POCKET

GARDENING
GUIDES

Cacti & Succulents

❖

DAVID SQUIRE

Illustrated by Vana Haggerty

TIGER BOOKS INTERNATIONAL
LONDON

Designed and conceived by

THE BRIDGEWATER BOOK COMPANY LTD

Art Directed by PETER BRIDGEWATER

Designed by TERRY JEAVONS

Illustrated by VANA HAGGERTY FLS

'Edited by MARGOT RICHARDSON

CLB 3372

This edition published in 1994 by

TIGER BOOKS INTERNATIONAL PLC, London

© 1994 Colour Library Books Ltd,

Godalming, Surrey

Printed and bound in Singapore

ISBN 1-85501-378-9

CONTENTS

WHAT ARE
CACTI AND SUCCULENTS?

❖

THESE are some of the most popular and widely grown houseplants in temperate areas. Although commonly and collectively known as 'cacti and succulents', this does cause confusion because, whilst they are all succulents, not all of them are cacti. Indeed, the only ones that are cacti are those that belong to the *Cactaceae* family. Apart from the botanical similarities in cacti flowers, they are characterized by having areoles. These resemble small pincushions from which spines, short hooks or long, woolly hairs grow. Another characteristic of the family is that, with the exception of Pereskias and young Opuntias, none of them bear leaves.

The other succulents are characterized by having fleshy stems and leaves which can store water, enabling them in their natural environment to survive periods of drought. Unlike cacti, which are all from one family, succulent plants come from many different ones. And not all plants within the same family are succulents. For example, the genus Senecio is in the *Compositae* family and contains annual, herbaceous and shrubby plants, as well as succulents such as String-of-Beads *(Senecio rowleyanus)* and the Gooseberry Kleinia *(Senecio herreianus)*.

Many of these plants have several botanical names and wherever possible these have been used.

DESERT *cacti are fascinating plants and can be grouped in a rectangular tray or round dish. Their wide range of shapes, sizes and textures creates spectacular displays throughout the year. Many develop flowers.*

THE CACTI *in this arrangement illustrate the huge variety of plants available. These desert types grow well on window sills and, despite their different shapes and sizes, all need well-drained compost.*

AFTER *a few years, some plants may dominate others and need to be planted into separate pots. This is best performed in spring, before the plants start into active growth. Avoid disturbing other plants.*

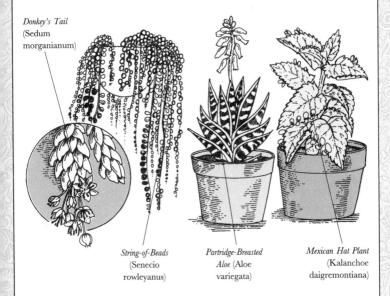

Donkey's Tail
(Sedum
morganianum)

String-of-Beads
(Senecio
rowleyanus)

Partridge-Breasted
Aloe (Aloe
variegata)

Mexican Hat Plant
(Kalanchoe
daigremontiana)

SUCCULENT *plants are varied in size and shape, some trailing and cascading while others create large, bushy features. Trailing types such as Donkey's Tail (Sedum morganianum) and String-of-Beads (Senecio rowleyanus) are ideal when positioned at the edge of a shelf or planted in an indoor hanging basket. Other succulents are better suited to growing in small pots. These include the variegated and stiff-leaved Partridge-breasted Aloe (Aloe variegata). Mexican hat plant (Kalanchoe daigremontiana) often grows 60cm/2ft or more high.*

DESERT AND FOREST CACTI

Cacti can be classified into two distinct types: desert types are native to warm, semi-desert areas of the American continent, while forest types come from forest regions of tropical America. An exception is the Mistletoe Cactus *(Rhipsalis baccifera)* which is native to Africa and Sri Lanka (earlier Ceylon), as well as from Florida to Brazil and Peru.

Forest cacti are distinguished from desert types by their trailing nature. Several of them, such as the Christmas Cactus *(Schlumbergera* 'Buckleyi'*)* and Easter Cactus *(Rhipsalidopsis gaertneri),* have flattened and segmented stems. Others, like the Mistletoe Cactus *(Rhipsalis baccifera),* have rounded stems, while the Chain Cactus *(Lepismium paradoxum)* has triangular, winged ones.

The well-known Rat's Tail Cactus *(Aporocactus flagelliformis)* has slender, rounded stems which although narrow resemble those of desert types. Indeed, it is better treated as a desert cactus than a forest one, which by nature it is.

Desert cacti live at ground level and take their nourishment from the soil, however impoverished it may appear in the wild. Forest types, however, live as epiphytes on the branches of trees. This means that, although they gain support from their host, they do not take nourishment in the way associated with parasitic plants such as Mistletoe.

7

BUYING CACTI
AND SUCCULENTS

❖

IN TEMPERATE climates, cacti and succulents are popular and widely grown houseplants. Indeed, nearly half of all homes have one or more of them. They are sold by garden centres and high street shops, but for a more comprehensive range it is necessary to buy them from specialist cacti and succulent nurseries. Some of these have mail order departments.

SELECTING PLANTS

Inspecting plants and what to look for when buying them is detailed below, but you should also give thought to where the plants will be displayed when you get them home. Both desert cacti and succulents are ideal for growing on window sills. If this is the only display area available for them, buy plants in small pots. This does not mean that they will all be the same height, since some epiphyllums

WHERE TO BUY

Cacti are 'specialist' plants which, as well as being sold by many garden centres, are available from cacti nurseries, either direct or by mail order. Horticultural associations often have sales of plants and these are usually of a good standard because they come from knowledgeable people.

Local high street garden shops and florists frequently have plants for sale, but do not buy those that are exposed to high or low temperature. Cold shocks to forest cacti may cause flower buds to fall off.

DO NOT *buy plants that are unlabelled. The presence of a label not only indicates the plant's name, but shows that someone has taken a pride in it. This is invariably reflected in the plant's health and appearance.*

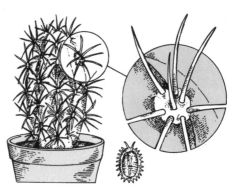

CHECK *plants to ensure they are not infested with pests or diseases. Look closely between and around spines since this is where many pests congregate. Check under pots to see if pests are visible in the drainage holes.*

WOOLLY *aphids and mealy bugs cluster around the base of spines on cacti. With succulent plants, it is the soft and tender parts that are most likely to be infested, especially around leaf joints and in crevices.*

(often known as Orchid Cacti) reach 45cm/18in or more high despite being best grown in small pots. However, do not use tall plants if the window has louvred blinds as these may damage the flowers. This is especially important when cacti and succulents are grown on kitchen windows: more than half of all houseplants are displayed there.

TAKING PLANTS HOME
Many plants are immediately damaged or may collapse later if badly treated during their journey home from a garden centre or nursery. Here are a few ways to safeguard them:

• Get the plants home as quickly as possible. Usually, buying plants from a nursery or garden centre is a special journey but, if bought from a high street shop, make it the last task of the outing.

• In a car, stand the plants in a box so that they cannot fall over, and preferably put them in a foot-well behind the front seats. Do not put them on seats in case you have to stop suddenly.

> ### ISOLATION WARD
>
> *When you get your new cacti or succulents home, do not immediately mix them with other plants. First, check them for the presence of pests and diseases. Then, as a pre-cautionary measure, isolate them for about ten days, checking them again for problems. If healthy, put them with existing plants; if contaminated, treat them in the appropriate way (see page 57).*

• Luggage compartments are often excessively hot during summer, or freezing in winter. Avoid both places: hot and dry places make plants wilt dramatically, while excessively cold ones may cause plants to collapse a week or so later.

• When you get your plants home, unpack them immediately and, if needed, water the compost. Allow excess moisture to drain, then place them in an 'isolation ward' (see above).

CHECK *that the outside of the pot or surface of the compost is not covered in slime or algae. This shows that the plant has been neglected and the roots may be congested within the pot, requiring repotting.*

DO NOT *buy a small plant in a large pot. Not only is it difficult to keep the compost evenly moist, but it suggests that the plant has only recently been repotted and is not get properly established.*

CHECK *that the plant is well secured in the compost: if it is leaning over and wobbles when the pot is picked up, do not buy it. It may have been only recently repotted. It may also be diseased.*

COMPOSTS AND POTTING

❖

Fifty or more years ago the range of recipes for composts for sowing seeds in and potting plants was so extensive that probably every nursery had a secret formula. Although they markedly varied in the amounts of loam (good topsoil), sharp sand, peat, decomposed farmyard manure and fertilizers used in them, individually they were a success because each person using them could tailor the necessary cultural requirements, such as firmness of potting and frequency of watering, to suit and so ensure success.

For example, several generations ago compost was literally rammed into a pot to provide plants with the maximum amount of compost a container would hold. This was thought to reduce the frequency of repotting and watering. Nowadays, loose potting is more the style, with the compost just being evenly firmed. This ensures better drainage and allows more air to enter the compost. But it needs frequent watering.

The range of composts suitable for cacti and succulents is detailed on the opposite page.

REPOTTING CACTI AND SUCCULENTS

All of these plants need to be repotted when their roots become congested, but there are slight differences between desert and forest cacti, also other succulents.

• <u>Desert cacti</u>: When young, repot them annually. In later years, this is only necessary when their roots fill the pot. This is best done in spring, transferring them into only slightly larger pots.

• <u>Forest cacti</u>: Repot annually, as soon as plants have finished flowering. However, Orchid Cacti (epiphyllums) are an exception since blooming is encouraged by keeping them in small pots and repotting them only when essential.

• <u>Other succulents</u>: Repot these plants in spring, but only when their root-balls are packed with roots. They grow well in shallow pots, rather than deep ones.

1. AFTER *seeds germinate they often grow in clusters, especially if sown too closely together. If left, they become drawn up, spindly and weak and never develop into strong, healthy plants, however well they are treated.*

2. CAREFULLY *transfer congested seedlings into pots or seed-trays, spacing them further apart. Use a small dibber to form a hole and, holding each seedling by a leaf, trail the roots in the hole and firm the compost.*

3. LIGHTLY *water the compost to settle it around the roots. Allow excess moisture to drain and then put the plants in light shade until established and growth resumes. Then, move them into brighter light.*

1. WHEN *cacti and succulents fill their pots with roots they must be transferred to larger ones. When repotting cacti, wrap several layers of newspaper around the stem to protect hands.*

2. INVERT *the pot while holding the plant secure and tap the rim on a firm surface so that the root-ball parts from the pot. Before repotting, gently tease out matted roots.*

3. PLACE *compost in the base of a slightly larger pot and position the root-ball on top, with its surface about 12mm/1/2in below the rim. Firm compost lightly but firmly around the root-ball.*

STEP-BY-STEP REPOTTING

Select a clean, dry pot, only fractionally larger than the present one. If using a clay pot, place a small piece of broken clay pot (crock), concave side downwards, over the hole. Also, for clay pots use a compost with a high proportion of loam.

If using plastic pots, there is no need to add a crock. Use a compost formed mainly of peat.

Remove the root-ball from the old pot (see above), tease out matted roots.

Place and lightly firm a small amount of compost in the pot's base, then position the root-ball on top. Ensure that there is a 12mm/1/2in space between the top of the root-ball and the pot's rim, so that the compost can be adequately watered.

Trickle compost between the root-ball and side of the pot and gently firm it. Add and firm further compost, but do not encroach upon the watering space. Then, label the plant (including the date of repotting) and gently fill up the watering space with clean water.

COMPOST MIXES

 Proprietary cactus and succulent composts are readily available, but it is possible to make your own. There are several recipes, all widely used, but most cactus specialists have their own tried and trusted one. Here are two mixtures to consider:

- *Four parts loam-based potting compost, two of moist peat and three of sharp grit.*
- *Two parts peat-based compost and one of sharp grit.*

If you are in doubt about the compost to use, consult with the nursery owner, who is usually pleased to give advice.

Whatever the mixture, it should not, after a few weeks, consolidate and prevent the entry of air; nor must it stop excess water from draining freely. These problems are likely to occur where high proportions of peat-based compost are used. Remember that desert cacti naturally live in well-drained compost.

CARING FOR DESERT CACTI

❖

THESE are cacti that naturally live in warm, semi-desert regions of the American continent. They are therefore accustomed to extremes of temperature between day and night. Here are the essential facts about growing them:

• <u>Light:</u> Position this type of cacti on a sunny window sill, especially in winter. In summer, light shading may be necessary in exceptionally hot situations. The alternative is to move them to a window sill away from direct sunlight.

• <u>Temperature:</u> Each species has its own needs but, in general, 10–13°C/50–55°F in winter is suitable, although many survive short periods down to 5°C/41°F. However, some hairy desert cacti, such as Old Man Cactus *(Cephalocereus senilis)* and Peruvian Old Man *(Espostoa lanata)*, need a minimum winter temperature of 15°C/59°F, or even a few degrees higher. In summer, temperatures rise dra-matically but light shading will help to protect plants from excessive heat. Give plants plenty of fresh air during summer.

• <u>Humidity:</u> No mist-spraying is needed for desert types, except for Cleistocactus species.

• <u>Feeding:</u> All desert cacti vary slightly in their need for food. Generally they benefit from a weak liquid fertilizer every two weeks from when their flower buds appear (often in mid to late spring, but depending on the species) until the onset of late summer. Use either a proprietary fertilizer specifically for cacti or a high potash type (often used for tomatoes in late summer). These feeds are especially important where peat-based composts are used, as they have little reserve of fertilizers.

• <u>Watering:</u> Water plants generously from mid-spring to late summer, keeping the compost moist but not totally and perpetually

BUNNY EARS (Opuntia microdasys) *belongs to a group widely known as Prickly Pears. This species has bright green, flattened stems dotted with tufts of yellow, barbed bristles. In the wild it bears yellow flowers; seldom in a pot.*

SUNSET CACTUS (Lobivia famatimensis) *has about twenty ribs which become densely covered with small clusters of yellow spines. The flowers, normally yellow, open for several days in succession, but close at night.*

GOLDEN BALL CACTUS (Notocactus leninghausii) *is slow growing, initially globular but later cylindrical, with yellow spines. From early to late summer it produces funnel-shaped, bright yellow, 2.5cm/1in wide flowers.*

POSITION *plants in full sun, especially in winter. However, during the hottest days of summer give protection from fierce sunlight by moving the plants or providing light shade.*

WATER *plants generously from mid-spring to late summer. In autumn, water sparingly and, during winter, give just sufficient to keep the compost barely moist to prevent plants from shrivelling.*

DO NOT *mist-spray desert cacti, except Cleistocactus types (a group that includes the well-known Silver Torch Cactus), but only when these are not in full and strong, continuous sunlight.*

saturated. From late summer, reduce the amount of water given to them until in mid to late autumn the compost is being kept almost dry. Take care, however, not to allow plants to shrivel.

• <u>Compost and repotting:</u> Repot only when the roots are congested (see pages 10 and 11 for details).

• <u>Propagation:</u> New plants can be raised from cuttings as well as seeds (see pages 18 to 23).

ENCOURAGING DESERT CACTI TO FLOWER

Desert cacti can be rather fickle at flowering, although the vast majority do bloom when young and certainly by the time they are three or four years old. This makes them ideal for displaying on window sills or in miniature cacti gardens in greenhouses.

The clue to their success is that most desert cacti will only develop flowers on new growths. It is therefore essential that plants are watered and fed adequately during summer to encourage growth that will bear flowers during the following year. But do not encourage growth by repotting established plants annually, as they

flower best when their roots are slightly congested.

Prickly Pears (Opuntias), however, are reluctant to develop flowers while small and especially when they are grown in small pot indoors on window sills.

VERSATILE OPUNTIAS

Opuntias are a large family of desert cacti native to much of the American continent. Some are prostrate, others tree-like.

Many have been introduced to other countries, such as Australia, India and South Africa, where they have grown rampantly and become serious pests.

Many have fruits which provide food. In the last century juices extracted from the fruits were used in Italy as water-colours, while in Mexico a drink known as colonche has long been prepared from them.

CARING FOR FOREST CACTI

❖

THESE are cacti that naturally live attached to branches of trees. Therefore, their needs are different from desert types. Here are the essential facts about successfully growing them:

• <u>Light:</u> They naturally grow on branches and with an overhead canopy of leaves that protects them from strong, direct light. Therefore, put them in a bright position but shaded from direct sunshine. Most forest cacti are grown in pots positioned at the edges of shelves so that their stems can trail. Alternatively, plant them in indoor hanging baskets – they look good in slatted types. Orchid Cactus (epiphyllums), however, can be grown in pots on window sills, but choose one that does not receive direct sunshine.

• <u>Temperature:</u> During their flowering and growing period, forest cacti thrive in anything from 13–21°C/55–70°F. While resting, however, 13–15°C/55–59°F is essential. The times of the flowering and resting periods vary from one species to another (see the

section on encouraging flowering on the opposite page).

• <u>Humidity:</u> Regularly mist-spray plants, but avoid moistening the flowers, as this causes decay.

• <u>Feeding:</u> During their growing period (see opposite page), forest cacti can be fed every two weeks with a weak liquid fertilizer, either a proprietary type specifically for cacti or a high potash type used for tomatoes during late summer.

• <u>Watering:</u> When these cacti are flowering, keep the compost evenly moist, but not continually saturated. Where possible, use clean rainwater; alternatively, especially in hardwater areas, use cooled, boiled tapwater. During each plant's resting period (see opposite page), keep the compost barely moist but, as this ends and buds start to form, slowly increase the frequency and amount of water .

• <u>Compost and repotting:</u> See pages 10 and 11 for details of compost. Repot forest cacti annually, shortly after they finish flowering. Orchid Cactus (epiphyllums), however, flower best when

CRAB CACTUS
(Schlumbergera truncata) *is well known for its mainly pink to deep red flowers that appear from late autumn to mid-winter. The edges of its flat, segmented stems are spiky.*

CHAIN CACTUS
(Lepismium paradoxum/ Rhipsalis paradoxa) *is distinctive, with triangular, segmented winged stems which are twisted at intervals. It is also widely known as the Link Plant.*

MISTLETOE CACTUS
(Rhipsalis baccifera/ R. cassutha) *has long, rounded stems and white flowers. These are followed by mistletoe-like fruits. In the wild it trails 6m/20ft or more from tall trees.*

POSITION *plants in good light but shaded from direct sun. The temperatures needed vary throughout the year and from one species to another. Mist-spray plants to create a humid atmosphere.*

THE *amount and frequency of water each plant needs changes throughout the year and according to whether it is flowering or resting. This radically differs between species (see below).*

MOST *forest cacti are repotted as soon as they cease flowering. Orchid Cacti (epiphyllums) are repotted less frequently since being pot-bound encourages the development of flowers.*

in pots where their roots are congested. Therefore, repot them every second or third year.

• <u>Propagation:</u> New plants can be raised from cuttings and by sowing seeds (see pages 18 to 21).

ENCOURAGING FOREST CACTI TO FLOWER

The most popular of these are the well-known Christmas Cactus *(Schlumbergera* 'Buckleyi'), Easter Cactus *(Rhipsalidopsis gaertneri/ Schlumbergera gaertneri)* and Orchid Cactus (epiphyllums).

The Rat's Tail Cactus *(Aporocactus flagelliformis)*, although a forest cactus, is best grown as a desert type (see pages 12 and 13).

• <u>Christmas Cactus:</u> Flowering is from late autumn to mid-winter and during this period keep the compost moist. From then until mid-spring the plant is in its resting stage and needs a cool temperature and less water. For the following couple of months until early summer keep the compost moist, then place the plant in a lightly shaded position outside during summer. In late summer move the plant indoors, keep cool and the compost dry until the

flower buds form. Then slightly increase the temperature and amount of water.

• <u>Easter Cactus:</u> Flowering is from early spring to late spring or early summer, and during this period keep the compost moist. During summer plants can be placed in a lightly shaded position outside. The resting period is from late summer to late winter, when plants need to be kept cool and the compost only just moist. From then until the flower buds form, usually in early spring, keep the compost barely moist and the temperature cool.

• <u>Orchid Cactus:</u> Flowering is from mid-spring to early or midsummer and during this period keep the compost moist and the plants in gentle warmth. After flowering, place outside in a lightly shaded position. In late summer, move them indoors and until early winter keep the compost moist. From then until late winter keep plants cool, about 10°C/ 50°F, and water infrequently. Then, keep the compost dry until flower buds form, when the temperature is increased and the compost watered more frequently.

CARING FOR SUCCULENTS

❖

ALL CACTI are succulent plants, but after removing both desert and forest types there remains a vast array of 'other succulents' with an amazing range of shapes and sizes. Many are ideal for growing in pots indoors, in greenhouses and conservatories.

An element of their success in the wild is an apparent tolerance of neglect, but do not take this as a clue to looking after them when they are grown as houseplants since they handsomely repay care and attention. Here are a few facts to help look after them:

• <u>Light</u>: A bright, sun-drenched window sill is ideal, although too fierce sunlight may damage some leaves. Therefore, in strong sunlight create light shade.

• <u>Temperature</u>: In winter, keep plants cool, 10–13°C/50–55°F, although they survive down to 5°C/41°F. In summer, normal room temperatures are adequate. Fresh air is essential, especially during hot summers.

GLAZING FACTOR

During winter, the type of glazing in windows radically influences the positioning of plants on window sills.

At night, temperatures directly inside single-glazed windows fall dramatically and if plants are trapped between drawn curtains and cold windows they may be damaged. If curtains are left open the plants are not at risk, except in an unheated room. Nevertheless, move them further into the room at night.

Placing plants in a shallow plastic or ceramic tray enables them to be moved quickly and easily. However, do not use trays more than 90cm/3ft long as the weight of plants may break them.

Where double-glazing is installed, there is less of a dramatic fall in temperature near windows.

AGAVE VICTORIAE-REGINAE *forms a dainty rosette of dark green leaves with attractive white markings. Additionally, each leaf has a black, spiny tip. It does not flower until eight or more years old.*

STRING OF BUTTONS (Crassula perfoliata) *is an unusual succulent shrub, in the wild reaching 60cm/2ft but much less when young and in a small pot indoors. The leaves, about 2.5cm/ 1in long, clasp the stem.*

MEXICAN SNOWBALL (Echeveria harmsii) *forms loose rosettes of leaves covered with downy hairs. The flowers are bell-shaped, scarlet and with yellow tips, which has encouraged the name Red Echeveria*

BRIGHT *light is essential, but avoid strong sunshine in summer as this could damage the surfaces of leaves. Succulents survive low winter temperatures, but avoid those below 5°C/41°F for long periods.*

ALTHOUGH *succulents are adapted to survive long periods without water, this does not produce the best plants. Therefore, in summer keep the compost evenly moist. In winter be less generous with water.*

REPOT *succulents in spring, but only when their root-balls are packed with roots. It is often necessary to remove the pot to check this. Water the compost afterwards to re-settle it around the roots.*

- <u>Humidity:</u> No mist-spraying is needed. Indeed, water spots on leaves during periods of high sunshine may cause damage to the surfaces of leaves.
- <u>Feeding:</u> From late spring to the beginning of late summer, feed plants every two weeks with a weak liquid fertilizer. Use a proprietary fertilizer specially prepared for cacti and succulents. Before applying fertilizers, water the compost. The combination of dry compost and strong fertilizers soon damages roots.
- <u>Watering:</u> Water plants generously during summer, whenever the compost shows signs of drying. Ensure the compost is well drained as waterlogging damages roots. In winter, keep the compost barely moist, especially if the temperature is likely to fall dramatically. A combination of low temperatures and wet compost are lethal to plants in winter.
- <u>Compost and repotting:</u> See pages 10 and 11 for details.
- <u>Propagation:</u> New plants can be raised from cuttings, as well as from seeds (see pages 18 to 21).

VETERINARY VALUE

The Cape Aloe (Aloe ferox), from Natal, grows 1.8m/6ft or more in the wild, but is much more reserved when young and indoors in a pot. It is a succulent plant which bears red flowers in terminal clusters on long stems in spring. It is also well known for a blackish material extracted from it, later purified and at one time extensively used in veterinary medicine.

The Soap Aloe (Aloe saponaria) from South Africa was used by the Zulus to treat scours (diarrhoea) in calves, stomach ailments in chickens, and to remove hair from hides.

Aloe ferox

SOWING CACTI SEEDS

❖

Sowing seeds is an easy way to raise cacti plants: some of them are sold in mixtures of several different types, others are just one species. A few of the many cacti that can be raised from seeds are described on the opposite page.

SOWING CACTI SEEDS

These are very varied plants and, therefore, the precise requirements for germination differ from one species to another. In general, however, sow seeds thinly and evenly on well-drained seed compost, preferably in spring but there is no reason why they cannot be sown at other times.

Prepare a small seed-pan or seed-tray in the way shown below. Most seeds are lightly covered with sieved seed compost, but specific instructions for each species are given on seed packets.

After watering by standing the container in water, allow excess moisture to drain, then cover with a plastic bag. Alternatively cover with a sheet of glass with newspaper over the top. Place the container in 20–25°C/68–77°F.

If the seeds are covered with glass and newspaper, remove the glass daily and wipe clear of water droplets. Then replace, together with the newspaper.

As soon as the seeds germinate, remove the newspaper.

Germination is sporadic and, although some seeds germinate in a few days, others take many weeks. During this period, water the compost by standing the container in a tray of water. If watered from above, seeds become washed over the surface.

It is often eight or more months before the seedlings are large enough to be transferred to small, individual pots.

> ### SUCCULENTS FROM SEEDS
>
> *Most succulent plants are easily raised from cuttings or division (see pages 20 to 23), but seeds of some are available, including Echeverias, Aloes, Agaves, Crassulas and Lithops.*

1. FILL *and lightly firm seed compost in the base and sides of a clean, dry, shallow seed-pan or seed-tray. Add more compost and use a straight-edged piece of wood to strike the compost level with the rim.*

2. USE *a round firmer or the flat top of a jar to firm the compost evenly so that it is about 12mm/1/2in below the rim. The surface must be level. Leaving this space allows for seeds to be lightly covered with compost.*

3. SPRINKLE *seeds into the V of a piece of folded card. Gently tap the card so that seeds fall evenly on the compost. Do not sow seeds within 12mm/1/2in of the sides as this is where compost first dries.*

CACTI TO RAISE FROM SEEDS

Many cacti can be raised from seeds. They are sold in mixtures as well as individual species. There are many of them, such as:

- Astrophytum mixture, including species such as Bishop's Cap (*A. myriostigma*), Silver Dollar (*A. asterias*) and Star Cactus (*A. ornatum*).

- Columnar, quick-growing types are specifically offered in some mixtures. These frequently reach 20cm/8in or more by the end of the second season.

- Echinocereus mixture includes a wide range of Hedgehog Cacti. These include cacti such as *E. dasyacanthus*, *E. fendleri*, *E. stramineus*, *E. melanocentrus* and *E. fitchii*.

- *Echinopsis* x 'New Abbeybrook Hybrids' are superb, flowering within two years of being sown and producing large flowers on small plants. Flower colours include scarlet, cream, gold, pink and white, as well as bicolors.

- Epiphyllums 'Hybrid Mixture' are the well-known Orchid Cacti. About two-and-a-half years after being sown they produce sweetly scented flowers in magenta, gold, cerise, scarlet and cream.

MANY *cacti can be easily grown from seeds, either of specific species or in mixtures.*

- *Lophophora williamsii* (Peyote/Dumpling Cactus) is unusual, forming an oval, spineless, blue-green body with light pink flowers.

- Mammillarias are well known, and mixtures include *M. bocasana*, *M. candida*, *M. guelzowiana*, *M. longiflora* and *M. pennispinosa*.

- Hairy Cacti are sold in mixtures of plants that produce shaggy, white hairs instead of spines. These seldom fail to fascinate children, and include *Cephalocereus senilis* (Old Man Cactus).

4. USE *a horticultural sieve to cover the seeds lightly with 3mm/¹/₈in of compost or sharp sand. Alternatively, use a coarse culinary type: but the flat-bottomed horticultural type is better as the covering is more even.*

5. PLACE *the sown container in a bowl shallowly filled with clean water. Moisture will seep to the compost's surface. Then, remove and allow excess water to drain. Draw a plastic bag over the seed-pan.*

6. ALTERNATIVELY, *place a piece of clear glass over the container and cover with a sheet of newspaper to create darkness. Remove the glass daily, wipe away condensation, turn upside-down and replace.*

RAISING PLANTS
FROM CUTTINGS

❖

AKING cuttings from cacti and other succulents and encouraging them to develop roots ensures that new plants are exactly the same as the parent. It is also a method that produces new plants quickly. Several types of cuttings are described here.

SUCCESSFUL CUTTINGS

Here are a few ideas that will make taking cuttings easier and ensure successful rooting.

• Cuttings can be taken throughout the year, but spring and early summer are the best times.

• Light and warmth are important when rooting cuttings, but strong light and high temperatures soon desiccate them. Cuttings are therefore much better when positioned in light shade and gentle warmth. Indoors and during summer, choose a window sill away from direct light.

• Moisture-retentive, well-aerated compost is essential and a mixture of equal parts moist peat and sharp sand is suitable. Sprinkle sharp sand on the compost's surface.

SMALL AND CIRCULAR LEAVES

A few succulents, including Sedum sieboldii *and its variegated forms, have small, circular, flat leaves that can be removed and laid flat on sandy but moisture-retentive compost.*

Cut off an entire stem at its base, then snap off individual leaves. Fill and firm a pot with compost, sprinkle sand on the surface and press leaves on it. Lightly water the compost and place the pot in shade and gentle warmth. When the cuttings develop roots and shoots, transfer them into small, individual pots.

• Do not insert cuttings within 12mm/^{1}/$_2$in of the pot's edge, as this is where compost first dries if watering is neglected.

• Label cuttings immediately they are inserted in compost. Record the date as well as the plant's common and botanical name.

1. CACTI *with clusters of small stems (around a mother plant or on their own) can be increased by using a sharp knife to sever them at compost level. Take care not to destroy the plant's shape when severing stems.*

2. LEAVE *the cut surfaces exposed to air for several days. Firm equal parts moist peat and sharp sand in a small pot. Sprinkle sharp sand on the surface. Make a hole 18–25mm/^{3}/$_4$–1in deep and insert a cutting.*

3. PUSH *the base of the cutting into the hole and firm compost around it. Gently water the compost from a watering can with a rose and place in light shade and gentle warmth. Avoid high temperatures.*

1. MOTHER-IN-LAW'S *tongue* (Sansevieria trifasciata) *can be increased from healthy, mature but relatively young leaves severed just below the compost's surface. Do not damage the plant's shape.*

2. USE *a sharp knife to cut each leaf into 5cm/2in long pieces. Avoid tearing them. Leave the cut surfaces to dry for a few days, and ensure that the top and bottom ends of the cuttings are not mixed up and confused.*

3. FILL *a seedtray with equal parts moist peat and sharp sand, then sprinkle sharp sand on the surface. Insert the base of each cutting 18mm/³/4in deep in the compost. Firm compost around their bases.*

• Take cuttings only from healthy plants that are good examples of their type. Thin and weak cuttings create poor plants, while pest- and disease-infested cuttings eventually spread these problems to established plants that are healthy.

• Always water plants the day before taking cuttings, so that the stems and leaves are firm and healthy.

• Ensure that while taking cuttings, the mother plant's shape is not ruined. Take cuttings evenly from around the entire plant. Also, do not leave short spurs; they are unsightly and encourage the onset of diseases.

• Use a sharp knife; blunt ones tear tissue, reducing the rate at which surfaces heal.

• Hormone rooting powders encourage the rapid development of roots. Some are combined with fungicides to reduce the risk of infections before roots form. Tip a small amount into a lid and dip the stem bases in it. Do not dip them directly into the can, as they may dampen and ruin the powder.

• When creating cuttings from prickly cacti, wear a pair of thin gardening gloves or rubber domestic types.

LEAF PROPAGATION

Many succulent plants have leaves that can be removed and encouraged to form roots by inserting them in moisture-retentive and well-aerated compost. Crassulas and echeverias are suitable types.

Remove leaves from a mature plant by gently bending them down until they snap off. Avoid spoiling the mother plant's shape. Fill and firm equal parts of moist peat and sharp sand in a pot, then sprinkle sharp sand on the surface. Allow the cut ends to dry for a few days, then insert several cuttings in a pot. Water and place the pot in gentle warmth until roots develop. Then, move rooted leaves into individual pots.

Jade Plant (Crassula argentea).

RAISING PLANTS BY DIVISION AND PLANTLETS

❖

NCREASING plants vegeta-
tively by division, cuttings or
plantlets ensures that they are
identical to the parent.

Some plants can be propagated
by both division and cuttings.
However, when the yellow-leaved
form of Mother-in-Law's Tongue
(*Sansevieria trifasciata* 'Laurentii') is
increased from leaf-cuttings (see
page 21), it reverts to the normal
type with dark green leaves mottled in grey. Therefore, it must be
propagated by division (right).

SUCCESSFUL DIVISION
• Water plants the day before
dividing them.
• While dividing plants, take the
opportunity to inspect their roots
for pests (see pages 56 and 57).
• Repot only healthy pieces from
around the outside of an old,
badly congested plant. Throw
away the inner part.
• It is better to divide plants into
several good-looking pieces than
to produce masses of small ones.

THE CHANDELIER PLANT

(Kalanchoe tubiflora/
Bryophyllum tubiflorum)
*develops plantlets at the ends of
tubular, succulent leaves. These
can be removed and encouraged
to form roots in exactly the same
way as for the Mexican Hat
(below). However, instead of
moving established plantlets into
individual pots, put three of the
Chandelier
Plant into a
7.5cm/3in
wide pot.*

*Chandelier
Plant*

• Use clean, dry pots and fresh
compost. Dirty pots may be infected with disease spores
• After repotting, water and place
the new plants in light shade and
gentle warmth until established.

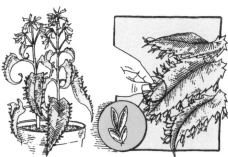

1. SEVERAL *succulent
plants develop plantlets
on their leaves. These can
be removed and encouraged
to develop roots. The Mexican
Hat* (Kalanchoe
daigremontiana) *produces
plantlets on its leaf edges.*

2. SELECT *a mature leaf
with several plantlets around
its edges and remove a few
of the largest ones. Do not
take the plantlets from just
one leaf or position, as this
may radically spoil the
plant's appearance.*

3. FILL *and lightly firm a
small pot with equal parts
moist peat and sharp sand.
Scatter the plantlets and
press them into the compost.
If they fall in clusters, use
the point of a knife to space
them out on the compost.*

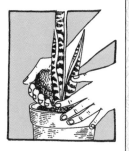

1. SUCCULENTS *with several stems arising at compost level can be increased by division. The yellow-edged form of Mother-in-Law's Tongue is increased by removing the pot and dividing the roots.*

2. DO NOT *excessively divide a plant, as the individual pieces will not then create attractive plants. Select a clean pot, place compost in the base, then position a plant so that it is at the same depth as before.*

3. PLACE *the plant in the centre of the pot and firm compost around it until 12mm/¹⁄₂in below the rim. Then, thoroughly water the compost to settle it around the roots, and place it in light shade until established.*

SUCCESSFUL PLANTLETS

• Use clean pots and fresh compost that is both moisture retentive and well aerated.

• Select mature plantlets just before they fall off a plant. At this stage they are large, but not woody, and have a good reserve of plant foods.

• Space plantlets out on the compost. When they are too close together, they compete for air, water and food, becoming weak and etiolated and never forming good plants.

• Press the plantlets into the surface of the compost.

• Do not allow the surface compost to dry out, as this damages the development of roots.

• Transfer rooted plantlets before they become congested.

4. STAND *the pot in a shallow tray of water until the surface is moist. Then remove and allow to drain. Place the pot on a lightly shaded window sill in gentle warmth. Keep the compost moist but not saturated.*

5. WHEN *the plantlets have rooted and are growing strongly, transfer them into small pots. Unlike the Chandelier Plant (see opposite page), only one plantlet of the Mexican Hat is put in each pot.*

6. USE *a watering can with a fine rose to water the plantlets. This will settle compost around the roots. Until plants are growing strongly, place them in light shade. Avoid strong and direct sunlight.*

DISPLAYING
CACTI AND SUCCULENTS

❖

MANY large cacti and other succulents create fascinating features when displayed on their own. Others are less dramatic in size and ideal for growing in trays on window sills, while trailing types are positioned either at the edges of shelves or planted in indoor hanging baskets.

IN POTS OR PLANTED?

Most cacti are grown and displayed in separate pots, while some can be planted in small groups in shallow dishes and other containers. Leaving plants in their own pots has its advantages: the compost can be watered specifically to suit the needs of each plant, which will vary throughout the year. Also, as plants grow they can be spaced further apart.

When planted in small groups in the same container, the compost is kept uniformly moist in

> ### PEBBLE POTS
>
> *A few succulent plants, known as living stones, have the appearance of pebbles. Lithops species are the main Pebble Plants or Living Stones, but there are others with a stone-like nature including Karoo Rose (Lapidaria margaretae) and Argyroderma and Conophytum species.*
>
> *These succulents can be planted in shallow pots or dishes, with the spaces around them covered with 6mm/1/4in of gravel chippings.*

summer and barely damp in winter. This may suit only some of the plants. Also, as they grow and intrude on each other they need to be removed and potted individually, often disturbing other plants.

WINDOW *sills are popular places for cacti and other succulents. Indeed, sunshine is essential and mirrors conditions in their natural environment. The wide range of these plants creates interest throughout the year.*

TRAILING *succulents are best displayed on small shelves in bright, sunny positions. Trailing forest cacti, however, must not be given direct sunlight. A shelf 1.2–1.5m/4–5ft from a sunny window is ideal.*

INDOOR *hanging baskets are excellent for forest cacti, enabling them to be seen from all sides and creating an environment similar to when they grow on trees. Use slatted baskets, as well as plastic types.*

VICTORIAN DISPLAYS

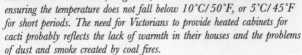

The Victorians were keen collectors of plants for gardens, windowboxes and displaying indoors. Wardian cases were introduced during the mid-1800s and parlour gardening became a pastime for many people.

Wardian cases were sealed, unheated environments in which plants such as ferns were grown. More lavish display cabinets include this round, heated type for cacti. Nowadays, cacti can be grown indoors throughout winter with little care other than, in general, ensuring the temperature does not fall below 10°C/50°F, or 5°C/45°F for short periods. The need for Victorians to provide heated cabinets for cacti probably reflects the lack of warmth in their houses and the problems of dust and smoke created by coal fires.

Desert cacti and small succulents can be grown in groups (until they outgrow each other), but do not mix forest types with them. Also, do not put a collection of forest types in the same container, as most of them need different resting and growing periods.

SPIKY AND PRICKLY

Most cacti are prickly, while some succulents have spiky tips to stiff leaves. These are fascinating features but to children can be dangerous, especially those at the toddling stage.

The succulent Mother-in-Law's Tongue *(Sansevieria trifasciata)* has leaves 75cm/2¹/₂ft or more long, rigid and with pointed tips. If children are present, display it on a window sill. When young and small, the Golden Barrel Cactus *(Echinocactus grusonii)* is ideal on a window sill: specimens 25cm/10in or more wide are available from specialist nurseries, but as they need a floor standing position are best avoided when toddlers or young children are around.

DISH GARDENS

Shallow, dish-like containers with attractive shapes form superb miniature cactus gardens. Because these containers do not usually have drainage holes, it is essential to cover their bases with pebbles or broken pieces of clay pots. Care is needed to ensure the compost is not watered excessively, especially in winter when they are resting.

Remove plants from their pots and plant them into equal parts loam-based potting compost and sharp sand or grit. Attractive rocks can be added to the design.

Bishop's Cap Cactus
(Astrophytum myriostigma)

SUCCULENTS FOR A WARM PATIO IN SUMMER

❖

DURING summer, many succulent plants can be placed outside on a sunny, wind-sheltered patio or terrace. They do, however, have to be returned indoors before temperatures fall below 5°C/41°F at night. Also, the compost in small pots in warm areas dries out quickly and several waterings a day may be necessary. Slugs and snails can be a problem and the regular use of baits is essential to protect plants.

Plants to consider include:

• *Agave americana* and its variegated forms are ideal, creating focal points around which other and smaller can be grouped.

• Several Crassulas create large, bushy, shrub-like features. *Crassula arborescens* (below) and the well-known Jade Plant *(C. argentea)* are two that are suitable.

• Many Sempervivums are robust enough outside all year in temperate and warmer areas and soon colonize dry walls and rock gardens. They are also good in pots.

PATIO OR TERRACE?

There are few 'real' patios in temperate regions. Indeed, we owe the term patio to the Spaniards, who used it to describe an inner court open to the sky and surrounded by a house. Nowadays (and mainly because estate agents like to glamorize all paved areas) any concreted area outside a house is known as a patio.

• Quick-growing, columnar desert cacti can be put outside in summer. Many are easily raised from seeds and by the end of their second season are 25cm/10in high. They revel in sunlight outdoors, but take them inside when the night temperature starts to drop.

THE SILVER JADE PLANT (Crassula arborescens) *forms a bushy shrub up to 3m/10ft high in the wild. In a pot on a patio in summer its rounded, grey-green leaves form an attractive feature.*

THE VARIEGATED CENTURY PLANT (Agave americana 'Marginata') *develops a large rosette of stiff, grey-green leaves with yellow edges. The ordinary type is also ideal on patios in summer.*

HEN-AND-CHICKENS (Sempervivum tectorum) *drenches pots with mid-green leaves that reveal maroon tips. There are several attractive forms to choose from. 'Commander Hay' has purple-red rosettes.*

FRUITS AND FOOD

❖

CACTI have long been valued for their sometimes edible fruits and various other useful properties. Such cacti include one of the largest, earlier known as *Cereus giganteus*, now *Carnegiea gigantea* and widely as Saguaro, Suwarrow and the Giant Cactus. It grows to 18m/60ft high and bears fruits 5–7.5cm/2–3in long, packed with black seeds embedded in crimson pulp. The Pimos and Papagos Indians turn them into a preserve.

Giant Cactus
(Carnegiea gigantea/
Cereus giganteus)

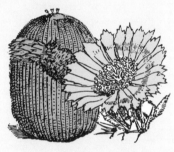

Echinocactus visnaga

The Central Mexican *Echinocactus visnaga* has large numbers of spines; in the 1870s one at the Royal Botanic Gardens, Kew, was estimated to have more than 17,000 spines. The Mexicans used the spines as toothpicks.

The Mule-Crippler Cactus or Eagle Claws *(Echinocactus horizonthalonius)* has stems with pulp that is made into confectionary.

Several members of the Barrel Cactus family provide food: the Turk's Head Cactus *(Ferocactus hamatacanthus)* from Southern Texas, New Mexico and northern Mexico develops fruits used locally as a substitute for lemons. While the Fish Hook Cactus *(Ferocactus wislizeni)* has edible pulp frequently used as a sweetmeat.

All Opuntias are known as Prickly Pears on account of their pear- or egg-shaped fruits, which are extensively eaten and greatly esteemed for their cooling qualities. They contain saccharin and, at one time in Naples, sugar was made from them.

One of the best known Opuntias is the Cochineal Plant *(Opuntia cochenillifera/Nopalea cochenillifera)*. This cactus was formerly cultivated for rearing the Mexican cochineal insect. The insects were later collected and used as the source of a scarlet dye.

The Beaver Tail or Rose Tuna *(O. basilaris)* has edible stems, flower buds and flowers.

Barbary Fig/Irish Mittens
(Opuntia vulgaris)

CACTI AND CHILDREN

❖

CACTI rarely fail to fascinate children, and a wide variety of miniature scenes can be created using cacti. They range from semi-deserts, peppered with model cowboys and Indians, to Japanese scenes where only a few small cacti and other succulents make a distinctive display. Even lunar landscapes with spacemen are a possibility.

DRAMATIC DISPLAYS

Displays of cacti can be created in long, shallow containers made of wood, terracotta or glassfibre and placed on window sills. But often these are used just to grow cacti in groups, rather than as a dramatic feature.

Sand and imitation grass (available from model shops), together with metal or plastic models of cowboys, Indians and horses, enliven desert scenes. Miniature figures, coloured gravels and tiny bridges are essential parts of Japanese displays. White gravel brightens displays and highlights plants; but use coloured gravels with care. Add coloured gravel in limited amounts, either to create paths or to indicate the edge of a feature within the display, or else the plants and models become secondary features.

VICTORIAN NOVELTY

Christmas-flowering cacti were frequently displayed in Victorian houses, but their low and trailing habit did not suit everyone. They therefore were often grafted on to the stems of the Barbados Gooseberry (Pereskia aculeata *– described and illustrated on page 30). A young plant was planted in a pot and tied to a cane to create a long stem, about 60cm/2ft high and clear of side shoots. Cuts were made at the top and several pieces of Christmas Cactus inserted and secured in the cuts. Some three to five years later a spectacular plant was created for displaying in a Victorian drawing room.*

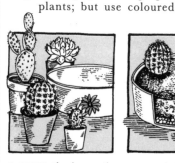

1. WHEN *planning a cacti garden, choose a few small cacti in various shapes and sizes. Do not pack the container with plants, as their unusual shapes should be clearly seen. Choose a shallow container.*

2. FILL *the base with clean shingle, then a layer of equal parts loam-based compost and grit. Position the plants so that the tops of their root-balls are about 12mm/1/2in below the rim of the container.*

3. GENTLY *firm compost around the root-balls, then add a thin layer of white, decorative gravel. This helps to create brightness and to highlight the plants. Lightly water the compost, but do not disturb the gravel.*

PLAYTIME WITH CACTI

Miniature desert scenes with upright as well as prickly and domed types of cacti frequently capture the attention of children. Adding model cowboys and Indians gives the scene further adventure and atmosphere. A few small rocks to create miniature cliffs add a further dimension. Gulleys and sandy slopes, together with mirrors that simulate ponds, produce a scene that introduces young people to the fascination of growing cacti.

GREENHOUSE DISPLAYS

Where a greenhouse is not being used, remove the staging on one or both sides and dig out the soil to a depth of 15cm/6in. Fill it with clean, broken bricks or rubble. Then, use wood or concrete slabs to build up the back to 30cm/12in high, and the front to 15cm/6in. Cover the rubble with 2.5cm/1in of 6mm/1/4in shingle, then fill and lightly firm the area with equal parts loam-based compost and grit. Creating a gentle slope allows the area to be landscaped and attractive rocks to be let into the surface to create a strata that looks natural.

Start planting from the back, using a few large cacti or succulents to create a backdrop for plants near the front. Use a mixture of desert cacti and other succulents; do not mix forest types with them.

Looking after these plants differs little from having them indoors, but here are a few clues to their success:

• During summer, paint the outside of the glass with a shading material, especially if the display faces strong sunlight.

• Ventilate the greenhouse freely during summer; avoid draughts.

• In winter, ensure that wind does not penetrate between panes of glass or through ill-fitting ventilators and doors.

• Ensure that water does not drip on plants, especially in winter.

• Water plants carefully in winter, when they are resting.

• From late spring to autumn, ensure that slugs cannot reach the plants. Spread gravel chippings on the compost to deter slugs, but also use baits.

• Do not let the temperature fall below 5°C/41°F in winter.

GEISHA GIRLS *and cacti initially appear to be an unusual combination, but they combine well in a simple, relatively uncluttered arrangement that uses just a few plants. A small white bridge and coloured gravels introduce further interest. Small mirrors can be used to simulate ornamental pools and streams*

EASY TO GROW CACTI
Aporocactus to Echinocereus
❖

THE RANGE of easy to grow cacti is wide and many of them are featured here and until pages 36 and 37. These are ideal cacti for beginners to start with and include trailing types as well as those that form rounded or columnar shapes in small pots on window sills. Most are grown for their attractive shapes, while others produce colourful flowers.

The care of desert cacti is detailed on pages 12 and 13, and forest ones on 14 and 15.

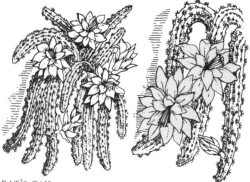

RAT'S TAIL CACTUS (Aporocactus flagelliformis) *is a forest cacti grown as a desert type. In spring it develops attractive cerise flowers.*

APOROCACTUS MALLISONII *is similar to the Rat's Tail Cactus, but with red flowers. It is ideal for planting in an indoor hanging basket.*

TORCH CACTUS (Cereus peruvianus) *forms a tall, blue-green, ribbed column often 75cm/2 1/2 ft or more high. When large it develops white flowers.*

PEANUT CACTUS (Chamaecereus silvestrii) *has spreading, bright green stems: small offsets look like peanuts. During spring and summer it bears brilliant scarlet flowers.*

THE UNUSUAL PERESKIAS

These are members of the Cactaceae family, but unlike the rest of them have leaves and a vine-like habit. However, the stems and branches are covered with spines, which enable them to cling to supports.

The best-known Pereskia is the Barbados Gooseberry (Pereskia aculeata), *which is native to an area from Florida to the Argentine.*

It grows 4.5m/15ft or more high and develops pear- or egg-shaped fruits, which are eaten fresh or preserved. The leaves are used as a vegetable.

Barbados Gooseberry (Pereskia aculeata)

SILVER TORCH
(Cleistocactus strausii) *eventually forms a column 1.8m/6ft high smothered in short, white spines that create a silver-like torch. During mid and late summer, mature plants become peppered with dark red, tubular flowers.*

ECHINOCEREUS PENTALOPHUS *is small, vigorous and sprawling, with 2.5cm/1in wide stems and bell-shaped, reddish-purple, large flowers during mid-summer. Ensure that the compost is well drained as the soft stems can rot.*

GOLDEN BARREL CACTUS (Echinocactus grusonii) *is grown for its round, barrel-like stance with rows of pale, golden-yellow spines. Only large, old plants develop yellow flowers, in rings at the plant's top.*

ECHINOCEREUS SALM-DYCKIANUS *eventually forms a mass of branching, ribbed stems with short, yellowish spines. In summer it bears large, funnel-shaped, orange flowers.*

BRAIN CACTUS (Echinofossulocactus lamellosus) *has a blue-green body with raised, wavy ribs and white, flattened spines. It develops pink, red-centred, tubular flowers in spring.*

ECHINOCEREUS WEBSTERIANUS *has a bright green body, densely covered with short, white spines borne in about twenty ribs. Large, lavender-pink flowers with green and yellow centres appear during summer.*

AFRICAN EXCEPTION

With the exception of the Mistletoe Cactus (now known as Rhipsalis baccifera, *but earlier as* R. cassutha), *cacti are native solely to the American continent. The Mistletoe Cactus, however, is also found growing in Africa and Sri Lanka (earlier Ceylon). In the wild, its cylindrical stems frequently trail up to 9m/30ft.*

EASY TO GROW CACTI
Echinopsis to Hamatocactus
❖

SEA-URCHIN CACTUS (Echinopsis
aurea) *forms a ribbed, cylindrical stem with
short spines. The scented, lemon-yellow flowers
appear mainly in late spring, then intermittently
throughout summer. Each opens during the
evening and lasts two or three days. It is also
known as* Lobivia aurea.

ECHINOPSIS
PARAMOUNT *Hybrid
'Orange Glory', another
Sea-urchin Cactus, is an
American Hybrid with deep,
glowing orange flowers
during summer. It is a cross
between Echinopsis and
Lobivia and develops a
cylindrical body peppered
with short spines.*

PINK EASTER LILY
(Echinopsis multiplex)
*has a green, barrel-like body
with twelve spiny ribs. The
scented, pink flowers, about
20cm/8in long, are produced
during summer.*

EPIPHYLLUM
'ACKERMANNII' *is an
Orchid Cactus, a forest type
and in need of special
attention (see pages 14 and
15). This is a well-known
variety, with brilliant red
flowers borne along the
edges of notched stems.*

EPIPHYLLUM 'COOPERI', *an
Orchid Cactus, has exquisite, lily-scented
white flowers up to 10cm/4in across.
These develop from low down on a
plant. It is a forest cacti and needs
special attention (see pages 14 and 15).*

CHIN CACTUS
(Gymnocalycium bruchii) *is small, with clusters of slightly curved, white spines. It is freely flowering, with satin-like pinkish blooms. Also sold as G. lafaldense.*

HIBOTAN CACTUS
(Gymnocalycium mihanovichii 'Hibotan') *is a novel type originated in Japan; it is grafted and resembles a tomato on a stout stick. It develops pink or white flowers.*

STRAWBERRY CACTUS (Hamatocactus setispinus) *has large yellow flowers borne amid clusters of attractive, long white spines. The blooms reveal reddish-orange centres and are borne during summer.*

CACTUS CONSERVATION

To aficionados of 'Western' films, a skyline peppered with tall cacti while a stage coach rattles over Indian Flats is essential. Moreover, 'Old Timers' are often seen escaping death by cutting open cacti to gain moisture. Today, desert cacti in North America are in need of protection from both vandals and people who dig them up in the hope of transplanting them into their gardens, perhaps alongside a patio.

If cacti are desired for garden decoration in suitable climates, always buy them from reputable nurseries for which they have been specially raised. In any case, cacti that are dug up from the wild have a low chance of survival when replanted. Before buying any large cacti, ask the nursery manager or owner for assurance that it was raised in a nursery and not dug up from the wild and then potted.

Giant Cactus
(Carnegiea gigantea/
Cereus giganteus)

EASY TO GROW CACTI
Lobivia to Opuntias

❖

COB CACTUS
(Lobivia hertrichiana)
*has a globular nature, with
bristly, spreading spines and
masses of spectacular bright
crimson flowers that are
borne even on young plants.*

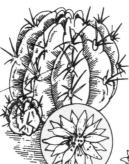

LADY FINGER CACTUS
(Mammillaria elongata)
*is formed of many finger-like
stems radiating from the
centre. During spring and
early summer it develops
masses of cream flowers.*

ROSE PINCUSHION
(Mammillaria
zeilmanniana) *initially has
a cylindrical stance, later
branching. In early summer
it bears masses of reddish-
violet flowers at its top and
around the sides.*

BALL CACTUS
(Notocactus ottonis) *has
a globular outline, with
spreading, yellow or brown,
slender spines. During early
and mid-summer it bears
yellow flowers, up to
10cm/4in long.*

MAGNIFICENT MAMMILLARIAS

*These cacti are even more prolific
than Opuntias, with perhaps three
hundred species, mainly native to
Mexico but also the West Indies, the
southern part of North America and
the northern part of South America.
They are ideal pot plants for
homes and are small enough to
be grouped on window sills.
Unlike most Opuntias grown
as pot plants, mammillarias
are treasured in homes for both*
*their flowers and attractive spines.
For example, the Snowball or
Pincushion Cactus (M. bocasana)
is smothered in fine white spines
and silky hairs. Also, M.
bombycina is densely
clad in white spines.*

Mammilllaria
bocasana

THE PROLIFIC OPUNTIAS

Few cacti are as distinctive as Opuntias, a group of cacti comprising more that two hundred species. Some are prostrate, while others are tree-like and 5.4m/18ft or more high. Their stems are jointed and, while most are pad-like and flat, some are cylindrical, such as in O. salmiana. *All species have barbed bristles (glochids) on each areole.*

As pot plants, they are better grown in conservatories, sunrooms and greenhouses than indoors.

Most do not flower in cultivation and are, therefore, grown mainly for their shapes, colourful pads and spines.

Most are increased by severing the pads at their joints, allowing them to dry for several days, then inserting in equal parts moist peat and sharp sand. Water the compost and place in gentle warmth.

Of all cacti, none have established themselves in so many countries other than their native America.

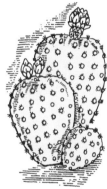

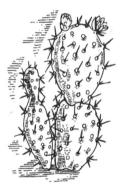

BEAVER-TAIL CACTUS (Opuntia basilaris) *is low and branching, with flattened, almost spineless stems. Unlike most Opuntias, it flowers early, with red flowers up to 5cm/2in wide.*

YELLOW BUNNY EARS (Opuntia microdasys) *is slow growing and bushy, with pale green pads 7.5–15cm/3–6in long. Plants in the wild develop very attractive yellow flowers.*

PRICKLY PEAR (Opuntia robusta) *grows to about 60cm/2ft high, with circular, blue-green pads peppered with yellow spines. It is better in a conservatory than indoors.*

CHOLLA CACTUS (Opuntia salmiana) *is sprawling and grows about 45cm/18in high with 12mm/^{1}/$_2$in wide cylindrical stems.*

PRICKLY PEAR (Opuntia scheerii) *is slow growing and seldom reaches above 75cm/2^1/$_2$ft in cultivation. The pads are covered with golden spines and hair.*

EASY TO GROW CACTI
Rebutia to Trichocereus

❖

CROWN CACTUS
(Rebutia albiflora) *has
beautiful white spines and
masses of satin-white flowers
in spring. These appear even
on small plants. Grow it in
a shallow pot.*

**REBUTIA CALLIANTHA
KRAINZIANA** *is another
Crown Cactus, with rings
of orange-red flowers in
spring. Ensure this plant is
positioned in bright sunshine
on a window sill.*

REBUTIA PYGMAEA
(formerly Lobivia
pygmaea) *forms a cluster of
finger-like stems with small,
needle-like spines and rose-
pink flowers. It is native to
Bolivia and northern Argentina.*

PERFECT HOUSEPLANTS

*Rebutias are generally known as
Crown Cacti and are native to
southern Bolivia and northern
Argentina. Many of them are ideal
for growing in small pots in homes,
sunrooms and conservatories.*

 *These plants are globular, some
forming clumps, and usually with
brilliantly coloured flowers, initially
trumpet-shaped, later flat.*

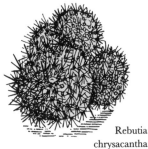

Rebutia
chrysacantha

*Mexican Sunball/
Red Crown (Rebutia minuscula)*

*Several flowers are borne at the
same time, each lasting about a
week. They open in the morning
and close at night.*

 *Most cacti bear flowers on new
growth at a plant's top. However,
Rebutias differ slightly and bloom
near and around their bases,
producing an attractive collar of
colour at their sides.*

SUCCULENT TWINER

The Rosary Vine (Ceropegia woodii) *is twining, creeping and trailing and markedly different from most other succulent plants. Also known as Heart's Entangled, String of Hearts, Hearts on a String and Heart Vine, it is ideal for planting in an indoor hanging basket. Pairs of heart-shaped, dark green leaves with silvery markings clasp purple stems which trail up to 90cm/3ft.*

The best leaf colourings are produced when plants are kept slightly dry. The flowers are purple and lantern-shaped. The whole plant is edible, while the tubers have been used as a pot vegetable.

Rosary Vine
(Ceropegia woodii)

FIRE-CROWN CACTUS (Rebutia senilis) *creates a spectacular display of red flowers in spring. It is further enhanced by silvery-white spines.*

CRAB OR CLAW CACTUS (Schlumbergera truncata/Zygocactus truncatus) *is a forest cact, with pink to red flowers from in autumn to winter.*

TRICHOCEREUS CHILENSIS *grows 7.5m/25ft high in the wild but is slow growing and ideal in a pot, where it forms a column of golden-brown spines. Only large plants develop flowers.*

WHITE TORCH CACTUS (Trichocereus spachianus) *eventually forms a column 90cm/3ft high and 6cm/2¹/2in wide. In a pot it is smaller, with greenish-white, night-opening flowers on large plants.*

TRICHOCEREUS CANDICANS *develops thick stems 60cm/2ft high and forms large clumps in the wild. In a pot it is less vigorous and has long, yellow spines. It bears 13cm/5in long, white flowers.*

MODERATELY
EASY TO GROW CACTI
Acanthocalycium to Ferocactus

❖

THESE are cacti that need slightly more care and attention than the easy to grow types featured on pages 30 to 37. However, they are still relatively easily grown on window sills indoors. Careful watering during winter is especially important as a combination of water-saturated compost and extremely low temperatures causes chills to roots and a shock for the entire plant. This often encourages the onset of decay, as well as disturbing the plant's normal resting and growth cycle. Also, avoid cold draughts.

VIOLET SEA-URCHIN (Acanthocalycium violaceum) *forms a rounded plant about 20cm/8in high and 13cm/5in thick, with needle-like, yellow spines up to 30mm/1¹/₄in long. During summer it develops very attractive lilac-coloured flowers at its top.*

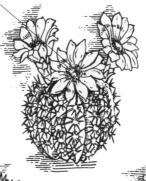

BISHOP'S HOOD (Astrophytum myriostigma), *also known as Bishop's Mitre and Monkshood, has a greyish body with four to eight prominent ribs. In summer it develops sweetly scented, yellow flowers. In the wild it grows 60cm/2ft high.*

BISHOP'S CAP CACTUS (Astrophytum ornatum) *has an attractive, dark green, rounded body divided into eight ribs and with amber-coloured spines. The sweetly scented yellow flowers do not appear until plants are about ten years old.*

BORZICACTUS AUREIFLORA (Matucana aureiflora) *is usually seen as a small, rounded but slightly flattened, plant. In the wild it can be 30cm/12in or more wide. During summer it bears bright yellow flowers.*

GIANT CACTUS (Carnegiea gigantea) *is extremely large, but takes more than two hundred years to reach 18m/60ft high. In a pot on a window sill it is usually 15cm/6in high, with a green and ribbed body bearing short spines. Only aged plants bear flowers.*

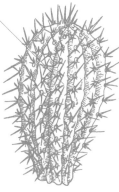

CORYPHANTHA VIVIPARA *belongs to a group of mainly small cacti. This species is globular and even in the wild reaches only 15cm/6in high and 8cm/3¹/₂in wide. The prominent white spines splay outwards in small, raised clusters. During summer it bears reddish flowers in clusters at its top.*

ECHINOCEREUS PERBELLUS *(sometimes listed as a variety of* E. reichenbachii, *the Lace Cactus) initially has a solitary nature but later forms a cluster. The ball-like stem elongates. The main attraction is the 5cm/2in wide, pink to purple flowers.*

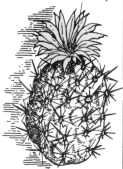

FEROCACTUS HORRIDUS *is another spine-clad species. The spines are in groups, each cluster having one that is long and hooked. Each plant has about twelve ribs. The yellow flowers are not normally borne on small plants. Nevertheless, the spines on their own create an attractive feature.*

DEVIL'S TONGUE (Ferocactus latispinus) *belongs to a group notorious for its ferocious spines. This species has wide and tapering, stiff and sharp, yellow spines with red tips. Hot and sunny late summers and early autumns encourage the development of purple-red flowers during autumn and early winter, even on plants only 10cm/4in wide.*

'FEROCIOUS' CACTI

Ferocactus means ferocious cacti and, therefore, it is not surprising that members of this genus have vicious spines, some straight or tapering, others hooked. There are about thirty-five species within this genus, all native to Mexico and the south-west states of North America. Some have edible fruits and stems. A few species can be grown indoors (see above and at left) on window sills, and their spines often become topics of conversation.

MODERATELY EASY TO GROW CACTI

Gymnocalycium to Notocactus

CHIN CACTUS (Gymnocalycium baldianum), *native to Argentina, forms a dark grey-green body with plenty of chin-like notches. During spring and summer it bears brilliant wine-red flowers about 36mm/1^1/2in wide. The tough spines are borne in clusters of three to seven.*

SPIDER CACTUS (Gymnocalycium denudatum) *has a rounded nature, up to 10cm/4in high and 15cm/6in wide in the wild, but smaller in a pot. Sharply pointed spines sparsely cover a rounded, deep green body. White to pale rose flowers appear in spring and early summer.*

GYMNOCALYCIUM HORRIDISPINUM *is another Chin Cactus, with a globular, dark green, shiny body with chin-like raised and depressed areas. The spines are borne in spreading clusters that create a ferocious appearance. Satin-pink flowers develop in spring and summer.*

THE COB CACTUS

Lobivias, native to Peru, Bolivia and Argentina, are collectively known as the Cob Cactus. They form round or cylindrical, medium-sized plants, usually with offsets around their bases, especially as they mature. During summer they develop brightly coloured, bell-shaped flowers. Each flower normally lasts for only a day or two, but fresh ones regularly appear. Some are moderately easy to grow, as described here, while others are easy; one is detailed on page 34. But there are others.

Lobivia jajoiana
(from northern Argentina)

COB CACTUS (Lobivia backebergii), *native to Bolivia, is diminutive and even in the wild only 10cm/4in high and 6cm/2^1/2in wide. The red, bell-shaped flowers appear in spring and summer.*

BEAUTIFUL BALL CACTUS

Notocactus species are widely known as the Ball Cactus, especially in North America. They are all native to South America, where initially they are spherical but later many become columnar and branching, some forming clumps. For example, Notocactus haselbergii *is globular, but* N. leninghausii *eventually develops a columnar stance.* N. mammulosus *is a globular type that remains solitary and bears yellow flowers at the plant's top.*

Notocactus mammulosus
(from Brazil, Uruguay and Argentina)

SUNSET CACTUS
(Lobivia densispina, *but sometimes sold as a variety of* L. famatimensis) *forms a clump of stems about 6cm/2¹/₂in high, densely covered in white spines. Yellow flowers are borne in summer.*

MAMMILLARIA
BOMBYCINA, *native to northern Mexico, forms a clump and is densely covered in needle-like, short spines. In late spring and early summer, red flowers appear in circles around the top of each stem.*

NEOPORTERIA
NAPINA, *native to Chile, forms stems about 2.5cm/ 1in wide and 7.5cm/3in high. Black spines are borne in small clusters on rounded ribs, with 2.5cm/1in wide bright yellow flowers in clusters at the plant's top.*

NEOPORTERIA NIDUS,
from Chile, develops dense clusters of spines on stems about 7.5cm/3in high and 6cm/ 2¹/₂in wide. Pink flowers cluster at the plant's top.

SCARLET BALL
CACTUS (Notocactus haselbergii) *has thirty or more ribs, each peppered with yellowish-white spines. Orange to red flowers appear on mature plants.*

MODERATELY
EASY TO GROW CACTI
Notocactus to Weingartia

❖

BALL CACTUS (Notocactus herteri) *forms a rounded, quick-growing plant, packed with reddish-brown spines peppered in clusters along raised ribs. During late summer it develops deep magenta flowers at its top.*

OLD MAN OF THE MOUNTAINS (Oreocereus celsianus) *is also known as* Borzicactus celsianus *and South American Old Man. Large specimens are covered in silky, white hairs. Only mature plants develop flowers.*

GOLDEN TOM-THUMB CACTUS (Parodia aureispina) *when young has a globular nature, later cylindrical and to about 20cm/8in high. During summer its top is densely covered with very attractive yellow flowers.*

PARODIA MICROSPERMA, *from northern Argentina, initially is rounded, later elongated. Its pale green body has whitish spines arranged along spiral ribs. In summer it develops yellow flowers.*

AN IMPRISONED CACTUS

Marie Antoinette, an Austrian princess and wife of Louis XVI of France, was tried for treason by the Revolutionary Tribunal and guillotined. However, when imprisoned, it is said that she sent for the Belgian artist Pierre-Joseph Redouté to paint a picture of a favourite cactus she had in her cell. Later, Redouté painted plants for Joséphine Bonaparte, in her then world-famous garden at Malmaison, near Paris.

ROYAL PATRONAGE

In the early part of the nineteenth century, many wealthy people in Britain devoted time and money to growing new and unusual plants. Mrs. Louisa Lawrence become one of the greatest amateur horticulturists of her generation and was famous for her royal soirées. In 1840, she invited Queen Victoria and the Prince Consort to see the blooms of a newly-introduced night-flowering cactus.

Albert, Prince Consort

PARODIA SANGUINIFLORA *is sometimes sold as a variety of* P. microsperma. *Initially it is globular, later cylindrical. Blood-red flowers appear in summer.*

REBUTIA muscula, *a Crown Cactus, is clump-forming, with rounded bodies densely covered with soft, white spines. During late spring and summer the tops of plants are peppered with orange flowers. This cactus should not be confused with* Rebutia minuscula, *the Red Crown Cactus.*

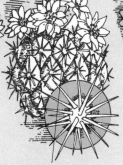

WEINGARTIA CUMINGII *(sometimes known as* Gymnocalycium neocumingii) *forms a small, spherical, bright green body peppered with white to yellow spines. During spring and summer it bears golden-yellow flowers.*

SULCOREBUTIA totorensis *develops brightly coloured, large, scarlet flowers around the sides of a globular body. Each flower lasts for three to five days, with flowering spread over four or five weeks. As plants mature they form large clumps packed with a large number of offsets.*

DIFFICULT TO GROW CACTI
Astrophytum to Thelocactus

SAND DOLLAR CACTUS
(Astrophytum asterias)
*belongs to a group widely
known as the Star Cactus. It
forms a flattened hemisphere
about 7.5cm/3in wide and
36mm/1¹/²in high. In
summer it develops very
attractive yellow, red-
throated, sweetly scented
flowers, 36mm/1¹/²in
wide, at its top.*

OLD MAN CACTUS
(Cephalocereus senilis)
*grows 12m/40ft or more in
the wild, but in a pot is
diminutive. The grey-green
body is peppered with yellow
spines which become covered
by long, silvery hairs. Only
old and large plants develop
flowers; nevertheless it is
a notable and very
attractive plant.*

COPIAPOA CINEREA,
*native to Chile, has a
chalky-white body peppered
with black spines, which
makes it well worth growing.
Unfortunately, it rarely
develops its 30mm/1¹/⁴in
wide, yellow flowers.
In a pot it often reaches
13cm/5in across. It is
a plant that never fails to
gain attention.*

STAR CACTI

*These are the well-known Astrophytums, a genus that includes four
widely grown species. They are all native to Mexico and three of
them are illustrated and described either on page 38 or above. But
another is the Goat's Horn Cactus
(Astrophytum capricorne). It grows up to
25cm/10in high and 13cm/5in wide. Its
body is light green and peppered with white,
woolly scales and seven or eight prominent ribs.
During summer it develops 5cm/2in wide
yellow flowers, each with a red centre.*

*The Bishop's Mitre Cactus (Astrophytum
myriostigma quadricostatum) has only
four ribs. It is a variation of the Bishop's
Hood Cactus (Astrophytum myriostigma)
which is featured on page 38.*

*Goat's Horn Cactus
(Astrophytum capricorne)*

GROWING DIFFICULT CACTI

Plenty of sunlight is essential for these cacti, together with well-drained compost that ensures excess water does not remain around the roots of plants. These cacti must have a resting period in winter, when the compost is kept barely moist. Additionally, regular feeding in summer ensures the development of young growths.

MAMMILLARIA PERBELLA, *from Central Mexico, grows to about 8cm/3¹/2in high and becomes covered in short, needle-like, white spines. In early summer it develops pink flowers in rings around the plant's top. Each petal has a beautiful carmine stripe down its centre.*

ECHINOCEREUS KNIPPELIANUS *is from Central Mexico, where it grows about 20cm/8in high. In a pot it is usually 7.5cm/3in high and forms a clump about 15cm/6in wide. During spring and early summer, this cactus develops pale pink flowers about 36mm/1¹/2in wide.*

PERUVIAN OLD MAN (Espostoa lanata), *also known as Snowball Cactus and Snowball, reaches 5.4m/18ft in its native northern Peru and southern Ecuador. Its body is covered with sharp spines and smothered by silky white hairs. Only large plants develop flowers.*

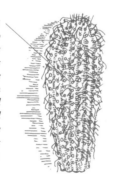

AGAVE CACTUS (Leuchtenbergia principis), *also known as Prism Cactus, comes from Mexico where it grows to 60cm/2ft high and 7.5cm/3in wide. The sweet but lightly fragrant yellow flowers, up to 10cm/4in wide, are handsome but unfortunately are not borne very freely.*

GLORY OF TEXAS (Thelocactus bicolor), *native of northern Mexico, is conical and in the wild grows 20cm/8in high and 7.5cm/3in wide. The spreading, stout spines are red with amber tips. During early summer it develops outstandingly attractive pale violet flowers, each with a richer-coloured, red throat.*

TALL AND
ERECT SUCCULENTS

◆

ANY succulent plants in the wild form shrubs 3m/10ft or more high, including the Tree Aloe *(Aloe arborescens)*, Jade Plant *(Crassula argentea)* and Velvet Elephant Ear *(Kalanchoe beharensis)*. When grown in pots in sunrooms, conservatories or indoors they are diminutive and seldom reach more than 60cm/2ft high. Others also have distinctive shapes, such as Mother-in-Law's Tongue *(Sansevieria trifasciata)* with stiff, sword-like leaves, and the Chandelier Plant *(Kalanchoe tubiflora)* about 90cm/3ft high.

AEONIUM ARBOREUM
'Nigrum' (also known as 'Zwartkop') is distinctive, with shiny, almost black, succulent leaves on branching stems. Unfortunately, it tends to loose its lower leaves, but nevertheless is worth growing.

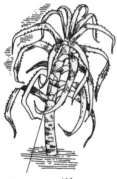

TREE ALOE (Aloe arborescens), *also known as Candelabra Aloe and Octopus Plant, is well branched, with saw-edged leaves about 20cm/8in long and slowly tapering to a curved tip. In the wild it reaches 3m/10ft high.*

JADE PLANT (Crassula argentea), *also known as Chinese Rubber Plant, Dollar Plant and Cauliflower Ears, forms a bushy shrub up to 60cm/2ft high when in a pot. It has branching stems and shiny, 2.5–5cm/1–2in long, green leaves.*

VELVET ELEPHANT EAR (Kalanchoe beharensis), *also known as Velvet Leaf, has somewhat triangular and heart-shaped, bright green leaves. Their surfaces have a velvet-like texture and are covered with brown hairs. In a pot it reaches about 60cm/2ft high; 3.6m/12ft in the wild.*

MEXICAN HAT (Kalanchoe daigremontiana), *also known as the Devil's Backbone, bears plantlets along the edges of its fleshy leaves (see pages 22 and 23 on how to encourage them to root).*

PANDA PLANT (Kalanchoe tomentosa), *the Plush Plant or Pussy Ears, is densely branched, with silvery and furry leaves.*

CHANDELIER PLANT (Kalanchoe tubiflora) *is distinctive, with tubular, channelled, spotted leaves bearing plantlets at their tips. These are easily encouraged to develop roots when placed on compost (see pages 22).*

CANDLE PLANT (Kleinia articulata/ Senecio articulatus), *also aptly known as Sausage Crassula and Hot Dog Cactus, has distinctive grey-green stems. The 5cm/2in long leaves are deeply lobed and borne in tufts.*

VARIEGATED MOTHER-IN-LAW'S TONGUE (Sansevieria trifasciata 'Laurentii') *is well known for its stiff, upright, sword-like leaves with cream-yellow stripes along their edges. It grows up to 45cm/1¹/₂ft high.*

PEN-WIPER PLANT

In addition to the Kalanchoes featured above, the Pen-wiper Kalanchoe (Kalanchoe marmorata) *from Ethiopia and Somalia is popular. Indeed, at one time it was known as* Kalanchoe *somaliensis, where it formed a glabrous shrub. It is ideal in a small pot indoors, growing about 25cm/10in high and with 10cm/4in long, blue-green, scalloped-edged leaves with chocolate-brown blotches. It sometimes develops white flowers in spring and early summer.*

Pen-wiper Kalanchoe (Kalanchoe marmorata)

ROSETTE-FORMING SUCCULENTS 1

❖

SUCCULENT plants that form neat rosettes are ideal houseplants. Most are grown for their attractive leaves, while some have the bonus of flowers borne on long stems. However, it is best to consider them as foliage plants, as that is their main contribution to room decoration.

In addition to the plants illustrated on these and the following two pages, there are many others, including:

• Golden Bird's Nest *(Sansevieria trifasciata* 'Golden Hahnii'/*S. hahnii* 'Variegata'): Golden variegated leaves about 10cm/4in long.

• Lace Aloe *(Aloe aristata)*: Stemless, grey-green, narrowly triangular leaves covered with white tubercles and with horny edges. Orange flowers are borne on 30cm/12in stems in early summer. The plant develops offsets.

• Ox Tongue *(Gasteria verrucosa)*: It is also well known as Warty Aloe and Rice Gasteria, and develops dull-green, wart-like white spots on succulent leaves up to 20cm/8in long.

• Saucer Plant *(Aeonium tabulaeforme)*: It forms a stemless, flat rosette of tightly packed, overlapping, pale green, waxy leaves.

• Tiger's Jaws *(Faucaria tigrina)*: Distinctive, stemless succulent, with 5cm/2in long, grey-green leaves peppered with white dots. Inward pointing, teeth-like bristles develop on the upper edges of the leaves. The 5cm/2in wide yellow flowers appear in clusters in summer and autumn.

• Zebra Haworthia *(Haworthia fasciata)*: Upright, slightly triangular, stiff and finely pointed, dark green leaves. They are covered with irregular bands of white tubercles.

CENTURY PLANT *(Agave americana) forms a large rosette of thick, stiff, grey-green leaves. Additionally, there are variegated forms: 'Mediopicta' has a yellow stripe down the centre of each leaf; 'Variegata' has stripes down the edges.*

THREAD AGAVE (Agave filifera) *grows 45cm/18in high, but usually is less than 25cm/10in in a pot. The shiny-green, stiff, tapering, spine-tipped leaves have horny tissue at their edges, later forming threads. Large plants bear flowers at the tops of long stems.*

AGAVE VICTORIAE-REGINAE *is a beautiful small plant, up to 25cm/10in high and with dark green, stiff leaves, edged in white and with black spines at their tips. It is less hardy than other Agaves and needs a minimum temperature of 10˚C/50˚F in winter.*

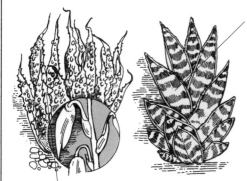

PARTRIDGE-BREASTED ALOE (Aloe variegata), *also known as Pheasant's Wings and Kanniedood Aloe, forms a mass of stemless, keeled leaves. The stiff, dark green, tooth-edged leaves have irregular bands of white across them, as well as white edges. During spring it bears orange flowers on stems about 25cm/10in long.*

HEDGEHOG ALOE (Aloe humilis), *also known as Spider Aloe and Crocodile Jaws, has 10cm/4in long, narrowly triangular, bluish-green leaves. They are attractively peppered with white tubercles. The edges are covered in white, tooth-like spines. Red flowers, tipped green, appear on 30cm/12in long stems.*

MOULDED WAX (Echeveria agavoides) *forms a neat rosette of pointed, stiff green leaves with brownish-red tips. Each leaf is up to 13cm/5in long, the longer ones around the outside and younger and shorter ones in the centre. Eventually, plants bear reddish flowers with yellow tips. It is native to Mexico.*

PURPLE CROWN (Aloe mitriformis), *also known as the Purple-and-Gold-Crown, has bright green, lance-shaped, tooth-edged leaves up to 20cm/8in long that form a loose rosette. With age, the edges of the leaves become horny and dark. This South African succulent develops scarlet flowers in dense heads on 60cm/2ft high stems.*

UNSAID MESSAGES

Without inking a pen or moving lips, the language of flowers expresses many thoughts, often from one lover to another. Cacti and succulents do not initially appear to be ideal messengers, although it is quite clear why cacti in general should imply warmth.

The Houseleek (Sempervivum tectorum), long associated with houses, is quite logic in its implied message of domestic industry and vivacity. Indeed, it is said to have been grown in pots since Roman times. Aloes have the unenviable task of symbolizing grief and religious superstition. A creeping Cereus tells of modest genius, while a night-blooming Cereus implies transient beauty.

Aloe

ROSETTE-FORMING
SUCCULENTS 2
❖

PAINTED LADY (Echeveria derenbergii) *forms a rosette 5–7.5cm/ 2–3in high and 7.5cm/3in wide, packed with pale green leaves that are covered in a white bloom. The leaves have attractive red edges. Orange flowers appear on 7.5cm/ 3in stems in early summer.*

PEARL PLANT (Haworthia margaritifera) *is a stemless and suckering succulent plant about 7.5cm/3in high. The dark green, initially upright then spreading, leaves are abundantly peppered with attractive white tubercles.*

BLUE ECHEVERIA (Echeveria glauca) is sometimes sold as Echeveria pumila glauca. *The glaucous-blue, waxy, spoon-shaped leaves form neat, somewhat flattened rosettes. Its stature makes it ideal for growing in a pot indoors.*

MEXICAN FIRECRACKER PLANT (Echeveria setosa) *creates an almost stemless rosette about 7.5cm/3in high and formed of succulent, red-tipped leaves. They are densely covered in soft, white hairs. During summer it develops very attractive red flowers on stems about 10cm/4in long.*

LIGHTNING PROTECTOR

It is not too surprising that the Houseleek (Sempervivum tectorum) was dedicated to Jupiter or Thor, or that it has been known as Thunderbear. During the eighth century Charlemagne, king of the Franks and later Charles 1, emperor of the Holy Roman Empire, ordered that Houseleeks should be planted on the roof of every house as protection against lightning and fire. Even during recent centuries, in many parts of Europe, Houseleeks were believed to give protection from thunder and lightning and to ensure prosperity.

FIBRE POWER

The Sansevieria Mother-in-Law's Tongue is well known to houseplant enthusiasts in temperate regions, but in the last two hundred years other species in tropical and sub-tropical regions have yielded fibres for use in sails, ropes, mats, hats, bowstrings and nets. They were also used in paper-making and locally for women to make skirts. The Ceylon Bowstring Hemp (S. zeylanica) was especially widely grown and in London in the mid-1920s was worth about £30 a ton.

Fibres for ropes and nets

STAR WINDOW PLANT (Haworthia tessellata) *is stemless, with somewhat triangular, 5cm/2in long, recurved and spreading, dark green leaves with transparent 'windows' on their upper surfaces. Also, the leaves are covered in pale green lines.*

BIRD'S NEST (Sansevieria hahnii, but sometimes sold as Sansevieria trifasciata hahnii) *forms a 15cm/ 6in high loose but neat rosette of grey and dark green leaves with attractive cross banding.*

COBWEB HOUSELEEK (Sempervivum arachnoideum), *also known as the Spider Houseleek, forms a low rosette spreading up to 25cm/10in wide. It becomes densely covered with cobweb-like, white threads. During early summer it develops bright, rose-red flowers.*

COMMON HOUSELEEK (Sempervivum tectorum), *also known as Hen-and-Chickens, is widely grown outdoors. It also forms an attractive houseplant. The spoon-shaped, bright to mid-green leaves form rosettes up to 7.5cm/3in high. During mid-summer it bears rose-purple flowers on 15–23cm/6–9in high stems.*

PEBBLE-LIKE SUCCULENTS

❖

THESE SMALL succulents are ideal for growing on bright sunny window sills. They resemble stones, and the most popular group is Lithops, the Pebble Plants or Living Stones. There are also Conophytum (known in North America as Cone Plant), Argyroderma and Lapidaria, which derives its name from the Latin for stones.

Grow these plants in equal parts loam-based compost and grit or sharp sand, with a layer of grit on the surface. During their resting periods, usually from late autumn to mid-spring (although this varies between species), the compost should be kept dry, with a minimum temperature of 5°C/41°F. In spring, water the compost thoroughly and position the plants in bright sunlight. Take care not to water plants excessively, as they may become bloated and subsequently decay. Ventilate plants well during summer, and repot them only every third year; in spring for Lithops and during the early part of mid-summer for Conophytums.

KAROO ROSE (Lapidaria margaretae), *native to south-west Africa, is formed of two, blue-grey, swollen leaves up to 36mm/1¹/2in high that form a deeply divided plant. The 5cm/2in wide flowers have golden-yellow upper sides.*

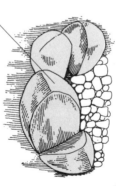

ARGYRODERMA TESTICULARE, *native to Cape Province, is formed of two greenish-white, swollen leaves that from a split-centred, stone-like plant about 30mm/1¹/4in high. The stemless flowers have white or cream petals.*

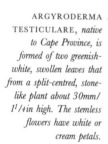

CONOPHYTUM BILOBUM *belongs to a group collectively known as Cone Plants. It forms a smooth-surfaced, two-lobed and somewhat heart-shaped, grey-green body about 5cm/2in high and 2.5cm/1in wide. During late summer and early autumn it bears 2.5cm/1in wide, daisy-like yellow flowers.*

PEBBLE PLANT
(Lithops bella) *is formed
of a pair of swollen, pale-
green leaves with darker
markings around their tops.
In early autumn it develops
nearly stemless, white, daisy-
like, fragrant flowers about
2.5cm/1in across.*

PEBBLE PLANT
(Lithops salicola) *has
a grey body with a green-
mottled top. Each is formed
of two swollen leaves, about
2.5cm/1in high, and either
solitary or in a large group.
The flowers are daisy-like,
white and 2.5cm/1in wide.*

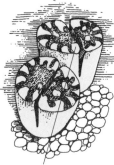

PEBBLE PLANT
(Lithops fulleri) *forms
clumps of two to six bodies,
each formed of two swollen,
dove-grey leaves with a violet
cast. Their tops are mottled
in dark brown. It bears
2.5cm/1in wide white
flowers.*

PEBBLE PLANT (Lithops
pseudotruncatella) *is
either solitary or clump-
forming. Each plant is
formed of a 30mm/1¹/₄in
high, grey-brown body with
brown lines and green dots.
There are several attractive
forms, including* alpina
*(yellow flowers in early
summer) and* mundtii
(late summer).

NATURE'S STONE

*Several groups of succulent plants mimic stones, but the best known group
is Lithops. Commonly, they are known as Pebble Plants, Living Stones,
Stonefaces, Flowering Stones and Mimicry Plants.
Lithops are native to south and south-west Africa
and normally grow in sandy-soil with just their
tops showing. Each plant is formed of a pair
of thickened, succulent leaves, which form a slit
across their top. Daisy-like, yellow or white
flowers appear through this channel.
Some species form clumps, others are
solitary. They are slow growing and need
plenty of light, especially during summer.*

Lithops marmorata

TRAILING
CACTI AND SUCCULENTS

❖

INDOOR plants that trail seldom fail to capture the attention, especially when they are growing in hanging baskets. In addition to the trailing cacti described here, others are featured on pages 14 and 15. They include the Rat's Tail Cactus *(Aporocactus flagelliformis)*, Chain Cactus *(Lepismium parodoxum)* and Mistletoe Cactus *(Rhipsalis baccifera)*. Trailing cacti are featured on the opposite page; other succulents on this page. Both types of plants are attractive, but while the succulents on this page are attractive throughout the year, cacti are best when in flower.

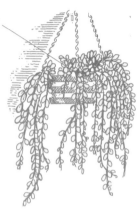

GOOSEBERRY KLEINIA (Senecio herreianus/ Kleinia herreiana) *develops oval, succulent, grape-like, green leaves on prostrate stems 45cm/18in or more long. It is best when allowed to trail and is ideal in a wooden-slatted, indoor hanging basket. It seldom flowers.*

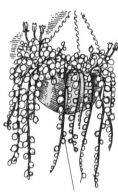

STRING-OF-BEADS (Senecio rowleyanus) *creates spectacular slender stems peppered with glaucous-green, succulent, grape-like leaves. The stems often trail for 60cm/2ft. Plant it in an indoor hanging basket, or a pot positioned on a shelf.*

DONKEY'S TAIL (Sedum morganianum), *also known as Burro's Tail, Beaver's Tail and Lamb's Tail, is ideal in a pot on a high shelf. Stems up to 60cm/2ft long are packed with fleshy, cylindrical, grey-green leaves, each about 18mm/ ³/4in long. From early to late summer it often bears pale pink flowers.*

SEDUM SIEBOLDII 'Medio-variegatum' *displays stemless, blue-green, flat, succulent leaves with cream centres. These are borne in threes along thin but strong, trailing stems. It is ideal for planting in a pot and positioning on a shelf. The ordinary species has all-green leaves and is sufficiently hardy to be grown in a hanging basket in a lobby, or outdoors in summer.*

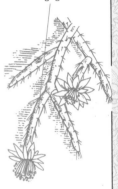

RHIPSALIS PILOCARPA (Erythrorhipsalis pilocarpa) *has a mass of trailing, cylindrical, dark green stems peppered with small, bushy spines. The scented, white or rose flowers appear in winter at the tips of long, trailing stems. It is ideal for planting in an indoor hanging basket.*

CHRISTMAS, EASTER OR CRAB CACTUS?

- <u>Crab Cactus</u> (Schlumbergera truncata): *Deeply spiked notches at the sides of flat stems.*
- <u>Christmas Cactus</u> (Schlumbergera 'Buckleyi'): *Rounded indentations on the edges.*
- <u>Easter Cactus</u> (Rhipsalidopsis gaertneri): *Dull green, flat stems with notched edges.*

BORZICACTUS AUREISPINUS (Loxanthocereus aureispinus/ Hildewintera aureispina) *has stems up to 50cm/20in long packed with bright golden spines. It branches from its base. Mature plants bear salmon-pink flowers. Grow it in a pot and position at the edge of a shelf, so that it trails.*

EASTER CACTUS (Rhipsalidopsis gaertneri/ Schlumbergera gaertneri) *has fleshy, flat, jointed stems that trail and bear bright-red flowers about 6cm/2¹/2in across in early and mid-spring. Plant it in an indoor hanging basket, or in a pot on a shelf.*

RHIPSALIDOPSIS ROSEA *(earlier known as* Rhipsalis rosea) *is upright at first, later pendulous. The greenish-red, segmented, freely-branching stems are usually flat. During late spring and early summer it develops scented, rose or pink flowers up to 5cm/2in wide. When young, place it on a sunny window sill.*

CHRISTMAS CACTUS (Schlumbergera 'Buckleyi') *is a hybrid between the Crab Cactus (S. truncata) and S. russelliana. Its mid-green, flat and segmented stems are untoothed. During winter and throughout Christmas it bears spectacular, rose or magenta-coloured, 5–7.5cm/2–3in long, flowers.*

PESTS, DISEASES AND PHYSIOLOGICAL DISORDERS
❖

ACTI appear to be well armed against pests, but it is often because they are profusely protected with spines that it is difficult to get at pests once they are established. Additionally, some pests have a protective covering of wax or wool that makes it difficult to eradicate them. Others infest roots and are not noticed until the plant wilts or the stems and leaves assume different colours.

Localized and small colonies of pests, especially if noticed early, can often be wiped away with cotton buds or swabs dipped in methylated spirit or rubbing alcohol. However, once infestations are large and established, controlling them even with chemicals can be impossible. Where an attack is severe, it is best to destroy the plant before it contaminates others. Always thoroughly read the instructions that accompany chemicals to ensure they will not damage the roots or stems of cacti or other succulents.

When buying cacti always inspect them carefully to ensure they are free from pests and diseases. Most of those bought from reputable nurseries will be clean; indeed, it is more likely that those from friends or plant sales will be contaminated and need treatment.

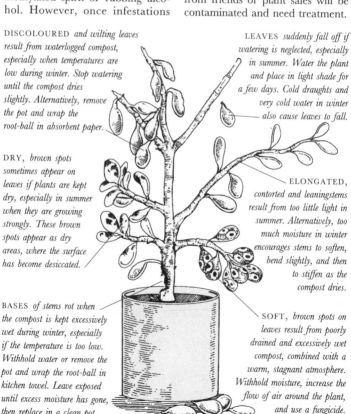

DISCOLOURED *and wilting leaves result from waterlogged compost, especially when temperatures are low during winter. Stop watering until the compost dries slightly. Alternatively, remove the pot and wrap the root-ball in absorbent paper.*

DRY, *brown spots sometimes appear on leaves if plants are kept dry, especially in summer when they are growing strongly. These brown spots appear as dry areas, where the surface has become desiccated.*

BASES *of stems rot when the compost is kept excessively wet during winter, especially if the temperature is too low. Withhold water or remove the pot and wrap the root-ball in kitchen towel. Leave exposed until excess moisture has gone, then replace in a clean pot.*

LEAVES *suddenly fall off if watering is neglected, especially in summer. Water the plant and place in light shade for a few days. Cold draughts and very cold water in winter also cause leaves to fall.*

ELONGATED, *contorted and leaning stems result from too little light in summer. Alternatively, too much moisture in winter encourages stems to soften, bend slightly, and then to stiffen as the compost dries.*

SOFT, *brown spots on leaves result from poorly drained and excessively wet compost, combined with a warm, stagnant atmosphere. Withhold moisture, increase the flow of air around the plant, and use a fungicide.*

CORKY SCAB *appears as rusty or corky sunken areas where cells have been killed, resulting from physical injury, drops in temperature or insect damage. There is no cure; burn infected plants.*

MEALY BUGS *feed on soft parts. Wipe off small clusters with cotton-swabs dipped in methylated spirits or rubbing alcohol. Also, use insecticides, but always burn severely infested plants.*

RED SPIDER MITES *occasionally infest cacti, causing mottling and webbing. Mist spraying is possible for succulent plants, otherwise use one of the systemic insecticides.*

ROOT KNOT EELWORMS *occasionally attack cacti and succulents, creating corky swellings on roots which disturb the intake of moisture and cause plants to collapse. Always destroy infected plants.*

ROOT MEALY BUGS *are closely related to mealy bugs but instead of attacking leaves and stems infest roots, causing discoloration and wilting. Drench the roots in an insecticide. Repeat the treatment several times.*

ROOT ROT *causes leaves to become yellow and wilt; the plant then collapses. It is a fungal decay caused by excessive watering and badly drained compost. Keep the compost dry; destroy badly infected plants.*

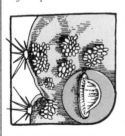

SCALE INSECTS *are mainly pests of neglected plants. They form swollen, protective, waxy-brown discs. Eradicate them in the same way as for mealy bugs. Do not hesitate to burn seriously infested plants.*

VIRUSES *invade some cacti, especially epiphyllums, causing yellow or, occasionally, purple spots. Viruses are impossible to eradicate from established plants. Always buy plants from reputable nurseries.*

WOOLLY APHIDS *resemble greenfly (aphids) covered with white, waxy wool. They get into soft joints around spines. Use an insecticide or a small brush dipped in methylated spirits or rubbing alcohol.*

FURTHER
SUCCULENTS TO CONSIDER

❖

N ADDITION to the many succulent plants, other than cacti, described throughout this book, there are others that are also superb in pots on window sills indoors. Those succulent plants already featured come from genera including Aloe, Agave and Echeveria, but there are many other popular and spectacular ones and these include Cotyledon, Euphorbia, Graptopetalum and Pachyphytum.

COTYLEDON

This is a genus of more than forty succulent plants and many of them are ideal for growing in greenhouses, conservatories and houses in temperate areas.

● Pig's Ears *(Cotyledon orbiculata)* grows up to 90cm/3ft high, with a shrubby, well-branched nature and bearing large, silvery-grey and red-edged leaves up to 13cm/5in long. During mid-summer it develops tubular, yellow and red flowers.

There are several attractive forms, including *Cotyledon orbiculata dinteri*, which is widely grown and with a compact body, making it ideal for small window sills. Another one, *C. o. oophylla*, has fleshy leaves covered in a white sheen

● Botterboom *(Cotyledon paniculata)* forms a shrub up to 1.8m/6ft high in its native south and south-west Africa. In a pot indoors it is usually 23cm/9in high, with a slow-growing, deciduous nature. The fleshy stem is swollen at its base, with the light green, spoon-shaped, 2.5cm/1in long leaves borne in late autumn. Occasionally it develops red, tubular flowers in mid-summer.

● Silver Ruffles *(Cotyledon undulata)*, also known as Silver Crown, is a distinctive succulent plant from southern Africa, somewhat similar to *Cotyledon orbiculata* and up to 60cm/2ft high. It develops a single, upright stem with thick and fleshy, wavy-edged, silvery-surfaced, evergreen leaves. From early to late summer it bears tubular, orange-yellow flowers about 18mm/³/₄in long.

EUPHORBIA

This is a group of more than two thousand species that range from annuals and herbaceous plants to succulents. Some are semi-succulent and include the well-known Crown of Thorns *(Euphorbia milii/ E. splendens)* from Madagascar. However, ones with a more succulent nature include the following.

● Turkish Temple *(Euphorbia obesa)* is better known in North America as the Living-Baseball and Gingham Golf-Ball. All of these common names indicate the plant's nature. Initially it is spherical but later cylindrical and up to 25cm/10in high. The leafless, grey-green stem is formed of eight, broad ribs. The small, but sweetly scented, bell-shaped green flowers are borne at the tops of plants during summer. Male and female flowers appear on separate plants.

● Milk Bush *(Euphorbia tirucalli)* is unusual and also widely known as the Indian Tree Spurge, Pencil Tree and Finger Tree. In its native tropical and southern Africa it forms a tree up to 10.5m/30ft high. In a pot it is a novelty, with succulent, leafless stems and milky, poisonous sap – avoid contact with cuts and eyes.

• *Euphorbia echinus* is also leafless and in its native Morocco forms a shrub up to 1.8m/6ft high. In a pot it rarely exceeds 90cm/3ft, with green stems that have wavy ridges and grey spines. Small, green flowers appear in mid-summer.

• *Euphorbia bupleurifolia* is not easy to grow and for that reason is rather rare. Nevertheless, with care (low temperatures and bright light during winter) it can be cultivated in greenhouses, conservatories and indoors, where it develops into a plant about 10cm/4in high. Its thick stem is attractively covered with warty tubercles. Tufts of leaves appear at each stem's top in spring, later falling.

• African Milk Barrel *(Euphorbia horrida)* is a deciduous, spiny shrub up to 90cm/3ft high in its native southern Africa. Its spiny nature initially makes it appear to be a true cactus, which it is not. In a pot indoors it is unlikely to exceed 20cm/8in high.

• Corkscrew *(Euphorbia mammillaris)*, from southern Africa, has a beautiful variegated form with a spiny, cactus nature. The deeply ribbed stems are variegated white. In a pot it seldom grows more than 20cm/8in high.

• *Euphorbia resinifera* forms a spiny shrub up to 1.8m/6ft high in its native Morocco. In a pot indoors it often reaches 30cm/12in high and forms clusters of bright green, four-angled stems. These are covered in short spines.

• Crown of Thorns *(Euphorbia milii/E. splendens)* is not a proper succulent. However, it has spines, is partially succulent and forms an ideal window sill plant when young. Later it needs a greenhouse or conservatory. It is also known as Christ Thorn and Christ Plant and in its native Madagascar has stems 1.2–1.8m/4–6ft high. In a pot indoors, or in a greenhouse or conservatory, it grows 30–60cm/1–2ft high and with a similar spread. It blooms at any time, especially during winter, with kidney-shaped, bright scarlet, flower-like bracts. The form 'Tananarive' has primrose-yellow bracts, fading to salmon-pink.

GRAPTOPETALUM

A group of about twelve species from Arizona and Mexico, and closely associated with echeverias. Several graptopetalums are ideal for growing indoors, in conservatories and greenhouses.

• Ghost Plant *(Graptopetalum paraguayensis)*, also known as Mother-of-Pearl Plant, forms a miniature, short-stemmed tree. The stems bear rosettes of thick, fleshy but brittle, greyish-green leaves with a silvery bloom. At first, rosettes of leaves appear on long, upright stems, but later these become prostrate.

• *Graptopetalum filiferum,* from Mexico, is stemless, with light green and rather greyish, spoon-shaped leaves.

PACHYPHYTUM

This is a small genus from Mexico and closely related to echeverias. Several of them are widely grown indoors, as well as in greenhouses and conservatories.

• Sugar Almond Plant *(Pachyphytum oviferum)* is also known as the Moonstone Plant on account of its fat, rounded, succulent leaves that are covered with a silvery-white bloom. They cluster tightly around rather lax stems. Unfortunately, during winter the lower leaves progressively shrivel. They are best removed to reduce the risk of diseases entering the plant. White, bell-like flowers appear in spring and are borne on short stalks above the leaves.

CACTI AND
SUCCULENT CALENDAR

SPRING

- Many cacti and succulents are bought in late spring. Inspect plants before buying them (8–9).
- Place newly bought plants in an 'isolation ward' for a few weeks until you are sure they are free from problems (9).
- Prepare for repotting plants in spring by ensuring a supply of suitable compost and clean pots (10–11).
- Repot cacti with congested roots (11). However, some cacti flower best when their roots are congested (10).
- Place desert cacti on a bright window sill in spring, but as brighter sunshine appears in late spring it may be necessary to provide light shading.
- During winter, desert cacti need a cool temperature. With the onset of spring, this can be allowed to rise gently (12–13). Ensure that the minimum is above 5°C/41°F, although for some hairy types the lowest temperature should be 15°C/ 59°F (12–13).
- During late spring, as better weather arrives, start to give desert cacti more water. Do not keep the compost continually saturated (12–13).
- In late spring, prepare for propagating (18–23).
- Place epiphyllums in good, but not strong and direct, light on window sills (14–15).
- Position forest cacti out of direct sunlight (14–15).
- Regularly mist-spray forest cacti, but avoid moistening the flowers (14–15).
- Water forest cacti (14–15).
- Feed forest cacti according to their individual needs (14–15).

SUMMER

- Inspect plants carefully before buying (8–9).
- Take care when taking plants home (9).
- Re-check plants for pests and diseases when you get them home. Place them in an 'isolation ward' for a few weeks until you are sure they are free from problems (9).
- In summer, desert cacti displayed on bright window sills may need light shading (12–13).
- Ensure desert cacti are given plenty of fresh air during summer (12–13).
- Feed desert cacti during summer, using a weak liquid fertilizer every two weeks (12). Alternatively, use a high potash tomato type.
- During summer, water desert cacti regularly, but ensure that the compost is not waterlogged. Good drainage is essential for these plants (12–13).
- In early summer, propagate cacti and succulents (18–23).
- Encourage desert cacti to develop flowers (13).
- Place epiphyllums in good, but not strong, direct light on window sills (14).
- Position forest cacti out of direct sunlight (14–15).
- Regularly mist-spray forest cacti, but avoid moistening the flowers (14–15).
- Water forest cacti with great care (14–15).
- Feed forest cacti according to their individual needs (14–15).
- Place succulents on window sills, but avoid excessively strong sunlight (16–17).
- Give succulents plenty of fresh air in summer (16).

AUTUMN

In autumn and winter, browse through seed catalogues and make notes of cacti and succulents for which seeds are available. Order them as soon as possible to ensure you are not disappointed during the following spring.

Do not move Christmas Cacti while their buds are forming or plants are flowering, as this encourages the buds or flowers to fall off. Put them in a bright but lightly shaded position in autumn, and leave them there until after they cease flowering.

- Place desert cacti on a bright window sill in autumn and winter (12–13).
- During autumn and winter, desert cacti need a cool temperature. For most cacti this is 10–13°C/50–55°F, although for short periods 5°C/41°F is acceptable. However, for hairy types the lowest temperature should be 15°C/59°F (13).
- In autumn, as the light intensity decreases and the temperature falls, give less water to desert cacti (12–13).
- Place epiphyllums in good light on a window sill, but avoid strong and direct light (14).
- Water and feed forest cacti with care and according to their individual needs (14–15).
- Regularly mist-spray forest cacti, but avoid moistening the flowers (14–15).
- Encourage forest-type cacti to flower (15).
- Place succulents on window sills, but avoid excessively strong sunlight (16–17).
- Place succulents (other than cacti) in a cool position, with a temperature of 10–13°C/50–55°F. However, many happily survive temperatures down to 5°C/41°F (16–17). High temeratures in autumn and winter are harmful.

WINTER

Desert cacti need radically different winter treatment to forest types. This is detailed on pages 12–15. The winter treatment of succulent plants, other than cacti, is detailed on pages 16–17. It is essential to differentiate between these types, and many plants are detailed on pages 30–55. Additionally, desert cacti are classified into three different groups (easy, moderate, and difficult to grow) to enable the right choices to be made, especially for those people new to growing cacti.

Succulent plants (other than cacti) are grouped according to their natures and where they will be displayed. For example, tall and erect ones are on pages 46–47, rosette-forming types on 48–51, pebble-like ones on 52–53, and trailing forms on 54.

- Place desert cacti on a bright window sill in winter (12–13).
- During winter, desert cacti need a cool temperature. For most cacti this is 10–13°C/50–55°F, although for short periods 5°C/41°F is adequate. However, for hairy types the lowest temperature should be 15°C/59°F (12–13).
- In winter, keep the compost in which desert cacti are growing almost dry, but ensure that the plants do not shrivel and become damaged (12–13).
- Place epiphyllums in good light (14).
- Water forest cacti with care during winter. This is influenced by the type (14–15).
- Place succulent plants on sunny window sills (16–17).
- Place succulents (other than cacti) in a cool position, with a temperature of 10–13°C/50–55°F. However, many happily survive temperatures down to 5°C/41°F (16–17).

USEFUL TERMS FOR
CACTI AND SUCCULENTS

❖

AREOLE: *A small, cushion-like area on the stem of a cacti from which arises slender, barbed hairs or spines known as glochids.*

BLEEDING: *The loss of sap from stems and leaves that have been cut.*

BLOOM: *This has two meanings: a collective term for flowers, and a waxy, powdery coating on the leaves of some plants. Many succulent plants reveal this attractive feature.*

CACTUS: *A member of the Cactaceae family and characterized by having areoles. Another feature of the family is that, with the exception of Pereskias and young Opuntias, none of them bear leaves.*

CHLOROSIS: *The yellowing or blanching of leaves due to lack of chlorophyll (the green colouring material in plants).*

CLONE: *A group of plants raised vegetatively from a single parent. All of them are exactly the same.*

COMPOST: *The material in which a plant's roots grow when in a pot. This may be loam-based (formed of a mixture of loam, peat and sharp sand), peat-based (mainly peat) or an environmentally friendly type created from coir, wood fibre or straw. The term also refers to decomposed vegetable material after it has been on a compost heap.*

CORKY SCAB: *Rusty or corky spots on stems and leaves, the result of damage (see page 57).*

CROCK: *A piece of broken clay pot placed concave-side downwards in the base of a clay pot to prevent compost from falling out or blocking the drainage hole. It is used only with loam-based composts and clay pots.*

CULTIVAR: *Short for cultivated variety and refers to a distinct variant in a species or hybrid that originated in cultivation, not in the wild.*

DAMPING OFF: *A fungal disease that causes seedlings to collapse at soil level. It usually attacks congested seedlings in seed-trays and pots, where the compost is kept excessively wet and the temperature too high.*

DESERT CACTI: *Their natural environment is warm, semi-desert regions in the American continent. They grow in soil at ground level.*

DIVISION: *A method of increasing plants by dividing the root part and separating it into two or more pieces.*

DORMANT PERIOD: *The period when a plant naturally stops growing. This is usually, but not always, during winter.*

EPIPHYTE: *A plant that grows above ground level, on another plant or even mossy rocks. Unlike parasites that live and feed on their hosts,* epiphytes only gain support. They usually live on debris that collects on branches or rocks. Forest cacti are epiphytes and invariably live on the branches of trees.

EXOTIC: *Properly, refers to any plant from a foreign (especially tropical) country, but has come to indicate plants with a colourful or unusual nature.*

FAMILY: *A group of similar plants encompassing one or more genera (plural of genus). A family name is distinguished by the ending -ae or -eae, such as* Cruciferae, *which is the cabbage family, or* Cactaceae *for cacti.*

FARINA: *Literally means flour and is used to describe the white, waxy powder on some leaves, stems and fruits.*

FOREST CACTI: *This group of cacti lives attached to trees. They do not take nourishment from their host, only support. Most forest cacti have a trailing nature. There are many more desert cacti than forest types.*

FUNGICIDE: *A substance used to control or prevent the onset of fungal diseases.*

GENUS: *A group of related plants and formed of one or more species. The plural of genus is genera.*

GLAUCOUS: *Describes the surface of leaves and stems when covered with a bluish-grey bloom.*

GLOCHID: *Small, slender, barbed hairs or spines which develop from areoles on cacti stems.*

HORMONES: *Chemical messengers that control physiological processes such as growth and flowering. They are also artificially used to encourage cuttings to develop roots.*

HYBRID: *The result of crossing two species or genera. A cross between two species is indicated by placing a cross between the generic and specific names. To indicate a cross between two genera, the cross is positioned before the first word of the botanical name.*

INFLORESCENCE: *The arrangement of flowers on a plant's stem.*

INSECTICIDE: *A substance used to kill insects.*

LATEX: *Milky sap, which exudes from cut surfaces of some plants. These include a several succulent plants, such as euphorbias.*

LOAM: *Good quality top-soil used, together with sharp sand and peat, to create loam-based compost.*

LOAM-BASED COMPOSTS: *See Loam.*

MEALY BUG: *a common insect on cacti. They resemble small, white woodlice (see page 57).*

MUTANT: *A deviation from the normal.*

NODE: *The position on a stem where a leaf or shoot joins it.*

OVER-POTTING: *Repotting a plant into a pot which is too large for it. When this happens, it is extremely difficult to keep the compost at the right degree of moisture.*

PEAT: *Frequently used with loam and sharp sand to form loam-based composts. It is also a major part of peat-based compost.*

PEAT-BASED COMPOSTS: *see Peat.*

POT-BOUND: *Describes the root-ball of a plant when congested with roots. At this stage it is repotted into a slightly larger pot and given more compost.*

POTTING-UP: *Transferring plants from one pot to another, so that they are given more space and compost in which to develop.*

PRICKING OFF/OUT: *Transferring seedlings from where they were sown into seed-trays or pots. This gives them extra space in which to develop and grow.*

REPOTTING: *Moving a plant growing in a pot and with congested roots into a larger pot.*

ROOT-BALL: *The area of soil around the roots of a plant in a pot.*

ROOT KNOT EELWORM: *They occasionally attack cacti, causing galls to appear on roots (see pages 57).*

ROOT MEALY BUGS: *They resemble small, white woodlice and infest roots (see pages 57).*

SPECIES: *A classification of plants within a genus.*

SUCCULENT: *A plant with thick, fleshy leaves or stems. These equip it to survive dry conditions. Within this overall grouping are cacti.*

SYSTEMIC: *A type of insecticide that is absorbed by the roots of a plant, making it toxic to insect pests. Take care that they are suitable for use on cacti and succulents.*

TOPDRESSING: *The replacement of surface soil in a pot with fresh compost. It is performed on plants when they become too large to be repotted.*

TRANSPIRATION: *The loss of moisture from the surface of leaves and stems. This is continual, but the rate depends on the plant.*

VARIETY: *A classification within a species and refers to a plant that originated naturally in the wild. However, it is commonly used to mean cultivars as well as varieties.*

VEGETATIVE PROPAGATION: *A method of increasing plants by taking cuttings, layering shoots and division, rather than by seeds.*

WOOLLY APHIDS: *These are related to greenfly (aphids), but covered in a protective, white, waxy wool (see page 57).*

XEROPHYTE: *A plant that is adapted to living in very dry conditions such as in a desert.*

INDEX